The Black Woman's
Little Book of

Magical Keys to Transforming Your Life

V.C. Alexander

Contents

Introduction

So you want to practice witchcraft—or maybe you want to strengthen your current practice? Well, this book is for you! After significant research, I've discovered there is there's an absolute dearth of spell books focusing on Black women and their specific issues. Don't worry, I've got you covered! In essence, my book offers effective practical spells that will help you with everything from getting quick cash through finding a side hustle to banishing toxic people from your life.

Specifically, this book will give you the necessary essentials to solve many of the common problems facing us as Black women. I won't promise that this book will address all your problems or cure cancer. And I certainly don't claim to be an expert or the most advanced witch. I'm far from it.

Actually, I just want to provide a helpful resource based on what I know. I understand that this book will probably be one of the many magic books you own, and that's how it should be. However, I hope that it functions as a valuable source of information and personal empowerment.

The spells in the book are definitely open to interpretation. Feel free to play around with them and make them your own. Substitutions, tweaks, and additions are encouraged. So, make the most of the material I've provided, and you may see a shift in your beliefs about your own capabilities.

Always remember the power is within you. You're pouring your own personal power into the works. Yes, you are powerful! Despite what society, your family, or your own self-doubts may tell you, you are powerful! So, it's time to harness that power to benefit your life!

How to Use This Book

I wanted to make this book as relatable, interesting, and informative as possible. I also aimed to make it easy to use.

It contains many anecdotes from my life (with some names and details changed to protect the innocent) to give you some background about why I created/used certain spells. These stories are simply for your enjoyment. I've included them because I hope they're entertaining. I also hope that they'll deeply resonate with you if you've ever faced similar situations as a Black woman. Another reason I included them is to show how you can help yourself with magic by using a little creativity and ingenuity. I hope that you peruse the spells as they could inspire you to create your own.

The book also integrates information and stories or myths about the different deities I've called on over the years. In some cases, this was done to give information and provide an understanding of why I chose these deities. In other cases, I included these myths because I found them fascinating and wanted to share them with you. Because I'm not an authority on ancient mythology, I consulted various sources to present these stories.

Regarding the spells and rituals, I tried to make them as clear as possible. I've included details on the materials used, the recommended/best timing to perform a ritual, and concise instructions. Each list of materials usually includes a short description of why those materials are used. I recommend that, as you add each item to your spell, you briefly hold it in your hand and think of its purpose in the spell. You should do this for two reasons:

1. The magic works because of you. You should know and understand why certain items are used, their powers, and what they symbolize. When you just add items to a spell without understanding why, you'll likely produce weak magic and obtain shoddy results.

2. You want to think of your purpose and charge that item with your intention so that it does its job.

Finally, I want you to know that you're free to experiment. In fact, I encourage you to do so. Yes, we share some commonalities as Black women. But everyone is unique—

with diverse wants, needs, and desires. Your magic should reflect your wants and needs. So, if burning petitions is something you don't like to do, then don't feel that you have to do so. Throw it into a flowing stream if you prefer. I've merely presented the rituals as I have used them. Take what's useful to you and work the magic!

Disclaimer: The Dangers of Magic and Self-Responsibility as a Witch

Ladies, magic is supposed to be fun. Being a witch and practicing witchcraft is a humbling and empowering experience. But I must warn you of the dangers of messing with magic before you dive into this book. Magic works. It works powerfully. But it doesn't always work in the way that you expect or hope for. Before you even attempt a spell you must understand this. There are things you can do to greatly reduce the risk but you need to understand that you are playing with powerful forces. Therefore it would benefit you to remember the following important points.

Firstly, to be successful when using magic you must have a certain level of self-mastery. What does that mean? Well you need mental and emotional stability. You'll require maturity and a sense of self-responsibility. When you decide to call on the forces of the universe in order to create, mold and sift energy to manifest your desires, you will see results. But without maturity or self-responsibility you will not know how to manage your creation. This could lead to disaster, to losing what you've created or losing far more than that. This could cause you to spiral into a dark pit of despair and hopelessness that may take years to recover from. I know this from experience. The key here is to know and understand yourself; know if you are willing to live up to the responsibilities of what you've requested. Know if you have some self-sabotaging behavior that could cause your dream to fall apart and be honest with yourself about if you are ready to have what you are asking for. If not, then do the work to make yourself ready before you cast a spell.

Secondly, it is necessary to be extremely clear about your intent and certain that you want the outcome you asked for. This is because spells do backfire and it is usually due to us not being clear about our intent. If you perform a spell to attract a new, handsome man into your life, you'd better be clear about all of the attributes you want and don't want. Or that handsome man could come with the trifecta; no job, kids and anger management issues. Be as detailed as possible when making your request because magic works and you get what you ask for.

Finally, sometimes your spells may seem to not work. You need to be balanced enough to understand that it happens. Not because magic doesn't work but because there may be some flaw in the equation. For example, you tried a spell during a new moon but unfortunately, you began the spell when the moon was void of course. Or you did a ritual for love but started on a Monday when a Friday may have worked best. These are just some examples as there are countless factors that could affect your magical workings. This is not said to discourage you, just to make you aware so that if it seems like a spell didn't work, you won't throw up your hands and say "witchcraft is bullshit!" Also, some spells work powerfully for some people and not at all for others. This is only natural, as we are all individuals with different levels of connection to the universe, our higher-selves, deities and the elements. It is important that you approach witchcraft and spell work like a scientist. Test out different methods, employ different variables and tweak your formulas to see what works best for you. But always remember to have fun!

Chapter 1

The Basics

The Time is right, the moment is here.
It is time to manifest my will.

*Y*OU are all you truly need to make magic work. Everything else is just symbolism. Rituals are used to focus energy to manifest your intentions.

Personal Mindset– Shifting Paradigms

There's one vital quality needed to be a powerful witch, one critical trait required to change your circumstances, and one major prerequisite for your spells to work. That vital quality is the correct mindset.

As Black women, we face many challenges that are unique to us. Whether in the workplace, in the classroom, or in relationships, our needs are multifaceted. This means that, yes you must work hard and smart to achieve your goals; however, magic can be a great supplement or boost. No, your life won't change overnight. But you can use magic to help finesse the outcome of any situation.

Black women are as worthy, lovable, and powerful as any other woman on this planet. We desire many of the same things most women want. And we deserve to have these needs met just like any other woman.

✯Visualization✯

Visualization is important and deeply connected to your mindset. In this book, you'll be asked many times to focus on your intention, not on your problem or need. You must believe that you're worthy of the result you desire and be able to see yourself in that situation. You must be able to see yourself, in that new home, with that car or at that new job, and experience the feelings of having them. You also have to know and believe that you're worthy and deserve it. Sit and really generate those feelings by putting yourself where you want to be and seeing yourself already having what you de- sire.

A Word on Results

There are many spell books on the market that are filled to the brim with spells for every occasion. Books on Hoodoo, Voodoo, Celtic magic, Wicca, the Orishas, and even demonology are readily available. So, what does this book offer that others don't? It offers you a Black woman's specific experience and personal perspective on witchcraft **and** on situations many Black women face.

With that being said, I won't tell you that every spell or working in this book will work for you specifically. Some spells work for some and not for others. Some spells work immediately and with dramatic results. Others are more subtle and may work slowly over time, until one day you look around and notice that your intention has manifested.

All I ask is that you use this book in good faith and set aside your skepticism. Set aside the "my momma/auntie/grandmother did it this way" thoughts and just try the magic. You may be pleasantly surprised. Despite the difference in methods or simplicity of the rituals, many may work for you.

Some people perform a ritual and then sit around waiting for the results, hoping that the spell has worked.

This is the wrong approach for a few reasons:

1. You need to do your part, too. If you wanted to earn more, would you just sit at home waiting for more money to fall into your lap? If you yearned to meet that special someone, would you just sit on your couch and pray for a man? No! You'd head out into the world trusting in your abilities, yourself, and your magic! If you want love, then you put yourself in places and situations where the magic can help you. If you desire a new job, you better send out applications, go on

interviews and network! You must do your part. So get off the couch!

2. Waiting for results is guaranteed to keep you doing just that, waiting for results. We've all heard about that cheesy law of attraction nonsense, right? Well, guess what, it's not completely stupid or completely wrong. Waiting for results will put out the vibrational frequency of waiting and attract more waiting for results. Trust! It's critical for you to trust that the magic has already worked, that the change you asked for has already manifested. After you perform any magic, you should trust in your power which leads me to...

3. The energy of hoping is detrimental to your magic. The energy of hoping feels too close to the energy of longing. And we only long for things we don't have. Your hoping is telling the universe that you're lacking, and it'll attract more lack. Say this statement and see how it feels: "I performed a spell and I hope it works." That statement is weak, shaky and whiny. That's a BS mentality to have. You must know that it has worked. Contrast it with this statement, "I performed a spell, and it has given me a new perspective." Or "I performed a spell, and I'm truly grateful that it is working." Or, even better, "I performed a spell and I'm grateful it worked!" ✶

✶What Type of (Black) Witch Are You?✶

I feel I need to address this topic here. When I started practicing witchcraft, it was later in life. After years of participating halfheartedly in Christianity, I came to a startling realization; I didn't believe one word of it, not one word. I'd wasted years in the church and had nothing tangible to show for it. I looked around and saw that I was well on my way to being one of those little old church ladies. You know the type: dressed to impress, a ridiculous hat, and always a fan for some reason. And as much as I loved and respected those church ladies, I knew that I didn't want to end up like them. I craved something different. I wanted to achieve my loftiest goals and desires in life. I wanted results!

So, I didn't come to the craft through my grandmother, auntie, or any relative. I felt drawn to it on my own. I came to it out of need, not tradition. And that significantly colors my approach to magic. I don't adhere to any one tradition. I'm interested in results and will utilize any means necessary. So, if I feel drawn to angel magic one day and Celtic magic the next, I'm at peace with that. It gets me results.

I can hear some of you saying- *'but why use white deities or Anglo traditions when you're writing for Black women?'* Well, it's **because** I'm writing for Black women. I want you to loosen your rigid ideas about what can and can't be done. I want Black women to know that all options, all paths, and all possibilities are open to them. So, don't pigeonhole yourself. Just go with the flow and see where it takes you.

With that being said, you should know some basics:

Herbs

I love using herbs in my spells. There's something about the smell and vibrations of various herbs. Indeed, herbs have been used for ages to cure all kinds of ailments, to soothe the mind, to give courage, and to protect. There are tons of spell books that have extensive lists of herbs, so I won't go into that here. Instead, what I'll do is tell you is that the herbs used are listed below the "You will need" section of each spell. I've also included the purpose of each herb in the spell so that you understand its significance in each ritual. This is important, you must hold each herb, focus your intent, then bless and empower it before adding it to the spell. Saying something simple such as, 'I bless and empower you by earth, air, fire and water to ...', will work wonders. Talk to the herbs and tell them what you want them to do. Finally, ladies you can find most of these in the supermarket! So, save your money and stock up at the grocery store.

Crystals and Stones

Many witches love their stones. And why wouldn't they? Stones, just like other magical implements, can carry a lot of power and can be employed in numerous ways. You can drop them into mojo bags, or you can charge them and use them as amulets. You can even bury them around your house to protect you from detrimental energies. And of course, you can charm them and wear them as jewelry. The possibilities are endless. You're constrained only by your creativity.

Although I do utilize them in my magic, I don't use stones as frequently as some other witches. So, I've provided a list here of my favorite stones and their uses. I think most of you have or should have a least three of these:

- ❀ Quartz crystal – peace, health, psychic awareness
- ❀ Rose quartz – love, peace
- ❀ Tiger's eye – money
- ❀ Amethyst – healing, spiritual protection, happiness, psychic awareness, dreams
- ❀ Agate – health, energy, luck
- ❀ Obsidian – protection
- ❀ Hematite – grounding, healing
- ❀ Sodalite – healing, wisdom
- ❀ Lapis Lazuli – joy, love, healing
- ❀ Citrine – money, protection
- ❀ Carnelian – courage, sexual energy
- ❀ Aventurine – luck, money, healing

This is just a short list. You can have many more or only three. The properties shown are only select qualities. There are many more uses for these crystals than those simply listed here.

Candles

We all know that candles are a staple. The imagery associated with witches usually depict a woman surrounded by candles as she casts a spell. It's deeply ingrained in our collective
consciousness. There's something inherently enthralling and magical about candles. Don't believe me? Well, try this

experiment; at night, turn off all lights, sit in a comfortable chair, strike a match, and light a candle. Now stare at the flame. Wondrous, isn't it? Notice how the flame dances and moves, notice how that tiny bit of light generates enough energy to light up the room. Now observe the heat it generates. If you stare deeply into the flame you may even see images. But that's an exercise for another time.

Candles, just like herbs and stones, are used to harness and channel power and focus intent. Different colors are utilized for different purposes; for example, green is for prosperity, pink for love, and red for passion or anger. Several spells in this book call for the use of candles. But you need to do more than just light the wick. You'll be asked to charge them, anoint/dress them, and even engrave your intent upon them. I love using spell candles and recommend that you stock up on many different colors. You can use votive, tea candles, seven-day candles, or whatever you have on hand. Here's a brief list of candle color correspondences:

- ❀ Black – banishing, protection, baneful magic
- ❀ White – general, all-purpose spirituality
- ❀ Yellow – communication
- ❀ Pink – love, romance and matters of the heart
- ❀ Orange – courage, achievement
- ❀ Red – lust, power, courage
- ❀ Blue – healing
- ❀ Green – money, growth
- ❀ Purple – power, spirituality

- Silver – psychic power, moon magic
- Gold – wealth, prosperity

Charging Candles

This couldn't be simpler. Sit in a quiet place. I like to do this at night in the dark because it lends it a more magical air. However, you can try it at any time of day. Take the candle in your hands and think intently about your purpose. Focus on the outcome you're aiming for, not the problem. Hold it in your hand and visualize psychic energy from your hands pouring into the candle along with your intent. You may even speak your intent through an incantation or a prayer over the candle as you hold it in your hands. Then visualize the candle glowing with psychic power and it is done. Your candle is now charged and ready for the next steps.

Engraving

Carving your intent onto a candle can really pack a punch. You can etch names or astrological symbols onto candles to designate a person or yourself in a working. If you want to draw certain things to you, like money, love, or wisdom just carve the words associated with your desires onto the candle. The same premise works for banishing. If you wish to banish a trait, habit, or undesired emotion, you can carve words that represent that thing onto your candle. You can really get creative with this.

Dressing/Anointing Candles

This can be as easy or complex as you'd like to make it. First, take the charged candle in hand and coat it in any oil of your choice. I love to use olive oil, but you can use any you desire—maybe a store-bought blend or even one you blended yourself. This is important: if you want to draw something to yourself, coat the candle from the wick downwards in sweeping motions toward yourself. Do the opposite if you want to banish something. Stroke upward in sweeping motions from the bottom of the candle to the wick, away from you. If it's a larger seven-day candle poke some holes into it, then coat the candle with the oil, keeping your intent firmly in mind throughout.

Next, on a plate, lay out any herbs you intend to use in the working and gently roll the oil-covered candle in the mixture, again thinking only of your intent as you do so. But, you may say, "My candle is in glass!" Just place the mixture on a paper and gently slide it onto the top of the glass candle. This process could get messy, so make sure that you have some paper towels available to clean up your hands.

Oils

Oils are multi-functional. You can use them to dress candles, anoint petitions or to anoint mojo bags.

They can be mixed with essential oils to create a unique perfume, astrological oil, or a blessing oil. Later in the book, we'll make a special oil you can wear or use in spells.

Care should always be taken when using essential oils. Some oils may be hazardous to pets, children, or pregnant women. Whether you use an oil mixture from this book, or you choose to create your own, it's solely your responsibility to investigate the dangers first.

Incense

I love to use incense in workings. Nothing stimulates the senses more than a beautiful fragrance. Smell is used to entice, to arouse, to calm and to cleanse. Much can be said about the use of incense in spell work. Did you know that you can focus your intent into incense just as you do with candles? I like to use stick and cone incense because they're easy and quick. But beware, many stores sell incense made with synthetic chemicals. Therefore, they carry none of the energies of the plant or material they claim to contain. However, the internet has made it simple and easy to find brands that offer the purest stick incense. I always have some on had to use in a spell or just to alter my mood. If all else fails, you can make your own. Making incenses can be simple or complicated. Mix herbs and resins to simulate your favorite scents.

The Moon

If you're not entirely certain about how to use the moon phases to perform magic, see the brief descriptions below:

1. The waxing moon – This is the best time to perform spells to draw things to you; for example, love, a job, friends or even a new car.

2. The waning moon – Align with this phase to perform hexes, curses, or any baneful magic. It's also the perfect time to banish things you no longer want in your life. For example, bad habits, negativity, bad luck or annoying people.

3. The new moon – During the new moon, you can perform magic that deals with new beginnings, growth or starting long-term goals.

Timing

Timing matters when we plan a spell. What do I mean by timing? Let's say you wish to perform a money/prosperity spell. Then you may consider beginning the spell on a Thursday or Friday. You could also take into consideration the phase of the moon. For example, you could begin the spell during the waxing moon to draw in that money. Additionally, you could include the astrological correspondence and perform the spell when the moon is in Taurus, Gemini, or Leo. Although some spells in this book recommend specific times, most do not. I'll leave it to your discretion to decide the best time.

Grounding, Centering, Casting Circles, and Calling Quarters

Before I start most work, I usually ground and center. What's grounding and centering? Well, grounding is a method used to connect yourself to the Earth and the world around you.

Centering is the act of bringing your awareness into your center.

I do it to clear my mind and put myself in the mood to perform a spell. It's essentially my way of saying, "now it's time to get into the zone." In most rituals, I'll say, "ground and center," but this is an optional step for you. If you feel you don't need it, it's perfectly all right to skip this step. If you choose to ground and center, please use whatever method you're most comfortable with applying. Using what works for you is always best.

If you need an example, I've included one below:

Grounding

1. Begin by turning off all electronics and communication devices.

2. Sit in a quiet place in a comfortable chair. Make sure your back is straight and that your feet are planted firmly on the floor.

3. Now take several deep breaths in through your nose and out through your mouth.

4. Once you feel settled, think about where you are and what you're doing. Where is your mind right now?

5. Now focus your consciousness on your inner world. Nothing else matters. Focus on what's going on inside you at this moment.

6. Take a deep breath in and imagine your feet sinking into the ground. Imagine them going deeper and deeper until you're planted firmly in the ground.

7. Now see roots growing from the bottom of your feet. Envision these roots slowly traveling deeper and deeper into the Earth until they reach the Earth's core.

8. Feel any unhelpful feelings and emotions flow out of you, down through your roots to be absorbed by the Earth

9. Next, see the warm energy from the Earth's core slowly traveling up through your roots and into your body. Sense your body glowing with that warm energy.

10. Know that you're grounded in your body and energized by the Earth.

✦ Circle Casting ✦ ❓❓

I like to cast a circle, and then call to the four quarters before I perform most spells. This is optional for you, although highly recommended. I know some who don't think it's strictly necessary. That is for you to decide because I'm not here to argue or try to convince anyone.

Why do we cast circles? You cast a circle for three primary reasons:

1. You're creating a sacred space where you can perform your rituals. You're setting this space apart from the mundane world and are entering the world of

magic. This signals the universe to pay attention to you and what you are doing.

2. You're containing the energy you raise in your ritual. You're focusing intently on your desired outcome and you want the energy you raise to be targeted solely on your goal. In addition, you may call on spirits and don't want any entities invoked to be released.

3. Finally, you'll want to keep out unwanted energies. You may have many different energies floating around you and your home. If allowed, they could adversely affect your spell in subtle but damaging ways.

There are many different ways to cast a circle. If you choose to cast a circle and call the quarters, I've included a simple method here for your convenience. This one was cribbed from Skye Alexander's great book '*Modern Witchcraft Grimoire: Your Complete Guide to Creating Your Own Book of Shadows.*' All you'll need is some incense and a bowl of saltwater.

To open the circle

1. Stand facing East. Dip your finger into the bowl of saltwater. Then, with your arm outstretched, sprinkle the water on the ground turning in a clockwise circle as you chant:

   With the power of Earth and Water, I cast this sacred circle.

2. Stop once you've returned to the East. Now imagine a wall of Earth and water surrounding you and separating you from the outside world.

3. Next, light your incense. With your arm outstretched, turn in a clockwise circle as you hold the incense and chant:

With the power of Fire and Air, I cast this sacred circle.

4. Once you've completed a full turn, imagine a wall of fire and air surrounding you, separating you from the outside.

It is done. Your circle has been cast.

To close the circle

1. Face East with your incense in hand. With your arm outstretched, turn in a counter-clockwise circle as you chant:

With the power of Fire and Air, I close this sacred circle.

2. Once you've completed a full turn, imagine the wall of fire and air dissolving around you.

3. Next, take your bowl of saltwater in hand. Dip your fingers into the water. Then, with your arm outstretched, sprinkle the water on the ground. Turn in a counter-clockwise circle as you chant:

With the power of Earth and Water, I close this sacred circle.

4. Stop once you've returned to the East. Then imagine the wall of Earth and water dissolving around you.

It is done.

✯ Calling the quarters ✯

1. Take a deep calming breath. Face East and say:

   Guardians of the East, I implore you to bring the spirit of air into this sacred space.

2. Face South and say:

   Guardians of the South, I implore you to bring the spirit of fire into this sacred space.

3. Face West and say:

   Guardians of the West, I implore you to bring the spirit of water into this sacred space.

4. Face North and say:

   Guardians of the North, I implore you to bring the spirit of Earth into this sacred space.

It is done.

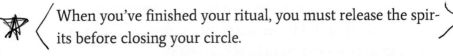 When you've finished your ritual, you must release the spirits before closing your circle.

1. Face East and say:

   Guardians of the East, I thank you and bid you farewell. Go in peace.

2. Face North and say:

   Guardians of the North, I thank you and bid you farewell. Go in peace.

3. Face West and say:

   Guardians of the West, I thank you and bid you farewell. Go in peace.

4. Face South and say:

   Guardians of the South, I thank you and bid you farewell. Go in peace.

Divination

Divination is the act of using a tool to receive information about future events. There are many methods that you can use to gain insight into the future. Some of my favorites are discussed below:

Pendulum Divination

This is one of the easiest forms of divination to get into. All you need to get started is a quartz crystal pendant hanging from a chain. Don't worry, since you can use anything to hang the crystal from: a string, a ribbon, a cord, or even a shoelace. Once you have your pendulum in hand, ask it to show you what "Yes" answers look like and what "No" answers look like. Then you simply ask yes/no questions and notice how the pendulum swings.

How does the pendulum receive this information? Your own psychic abilities act on the pendulum. It is believed that we all possess some level of innate psychic ability. And, by using the pendulum as a conduit, you can tap into your psychic abilities. Because of its simplicity, I suggest that you try it as soon as possible.

Scrying

When you think of the word "scrying," what images come to mind? Is it an image of a mysterious gypsy woman, layered in colorful scarves, eyes rimmed heavily with black eyeliner, fingers curling over a crystal ball? Or maybe an ugly old crone of a witch, cackling malevolently as she spies on an unwitting target? So, is that what scrying is? Yes and no.

You can use crystal balls for scrying, but not the ones you find in gift shops at the mall. A real genuine ball made of pure crystal. The problem is that you'll have to throw down a lot of cash to purchase an authentic one. You can use a black mirror purchased from an occult store, or you can make one yourself using an ordinary mirror and some black paint. However, a simpler method utilizes a bowl of water to gaze into intently. Whatever you choose to use, the process is the same. Sit in a quiet dark place, clear your mind, and gaze unfocusedly into the object. Let whatever images you notice rise to the surface. Often you may find answers to questions you didn't even know you had.

Tarot

The tarot is a favorite form of divination for me. I love everything about it. I adore the way each card looks. I love gazing at a card and trying to decipher the hidden meaning behind each symbol. And of course, I love the different varieties of tarot cards. There are many to choose from, such as the Rider-Waite-Smith Deck, Thoth decks, goddess-inspired decks, cat decks, Orisha decks, Egyptian god decks. The varieties are limitless!

So how do tarot cards work? The tarot uses symbolism. For me, simply gazing at a tarot card sparks numerous associations and reactions in my mind. Because of their symbolism, tarot cards are great for use in spells. They can be used to symbolize you, your desires, your fears, or your aspirations. In fact, this book contains several spells that incorporate tarot cards. In each of these spells, I briefly explain the significance of each card and why it is used. Remember, you're encouraged to experiment. So, if you prefer to swap out cards, go right ahead. It's your magic!

Chapter 2

Spells for Your Wellbeing

Nothing can hold me back,
my path is now clear.

Wellbeing is so important and necessary to our lives, but it can be difficult to maintain. Years ago, I was down and out mentally and physically. I was suffering from low self-esteem. I was often left feeling hurt, angry, and depressed about all of the shenanigans and tomfoolery I had to go through as a Black woman climbing the corporate ladder to success. On top of that, I found out my mother had breast cancer. That was the blow that really sent me spiraling as my mother and I are very close. I was at my wit's end trying to be strong for her, worrying about her treatment, the cost of procedures, and the toll it'd take on her. And, of course, I was concerned about losing her.

So many Black women have faced similar problems. We're often out in the world on our own and sent on a mission to seek out success at all costs. We frequently have to juggle the responsibility of family, being caregivers, and being the glue that holds our community together.

But I want us to stop and think: what help can I be to others if I can't help myself? What good can you do for yourself or your family if you don't cultivate and maintain a feeling of wellness in yourself? Put away superwoman, toss aside the need to always be strong, and engage in some magical and mystical self-care!

Yemoja Bath

Nothing beats stripping away the armor of the day and sinking into a nice relaxing bath. Soaking in the lightly scented water quickly puts your mind at ease. All of your problems, tensions, and concerns simply float away. It's then, when your mind is calm and at ease, that you're finally able to gain a sense of clarity. I find that all kinds of ideas flow through my mind whenever I am soaking in water. So, here's a simple bath ritual to help put your mind at ease (because simplicity works!) The power of Yemoja will help to calm you and give you a general feeling of wellbeing.

Who is Yemoja? Yemoja is the Orisha (spirit) of the sea in the Yoruba religion. She shares this responsibility with Olokun. While Yemoja governs the upper half of the ocean, Olokun governs depths. She is said to have given birth to many of the other Orishas. Therefore, she's closely associated with motherhood, nurturing, and sustenance. Her colors are blue and white. Her symbols include seashells, cowrie shells, conch shells, or anything from the sea. We'll be using her energy to add nurturing vibrations to this bath.

You will need

- A blue sachet
- Any one of the following: pearls, blue topaz, aquamarine, blue lace agate, or mother of pearl
- Cornflower petals (or petals from any blue flower)
- Gardenia petals – for peace
- Thyme – for health and healing
- Lavender – for happiness and peace
- Rosemary, which is also called Dew of the Sea – for healing, purification, and mental powers
- Marjoram – for happiness, health, and protection
- 4 small blue votive candles
- 3 small white candles

Procedure

1. Add the thyme, rosemary, stone of your choice, and cowry shells to the blue sachet.

2. Fill a tub with water and place the sachet in the tub.

3. Add in the blue and white flowers and let their essence infuse the water.

4. Place the blue and white candles in an alternating pattern around the tub.

5. Light the candles.

6. Place your hand into the water, saying:

Yemoja, Yemayá, Iemoja mother of all living things, she who rules over motherhood and owns all the waters of the Earth. She who gave birth to the stars, the moon, the sun and most of the Orishas, I call to you. Send your nurturing spirit, Oh Yemoja, goddess of nourishment and of sustenance. I thank you for your assistance.

7. Allow yourself to slip into the bath. As you sit in the bath, you may chant the following:

Yemoja, fill me with your calming energy.
Cleanse away all stress and negativity.
Yemoja, Yemoja, bring calm and clarity!

8. Soak in the tub for 15-30 minutes or until you're ready to leave. Don't towel off, allow the water of the bath to dry on your skin.

Blessed Home Floor Wash

Recently, I noticed that I felt stuck and in a rut. Nothing was wrong per se, but my overall energy was low. I couldn't put my finger on the exact cause because everything in my life seemed normal. I started feeling the need to get away, to get out of the house. So, I increased my outdoor activities. I went out for long walks, caught up with friends, and indulged in some sightseeing, among other things. As a result, it worked! During these times, my mood was miraculously lifted. However, upon returning to my home the low energy feeling would hit me again. It was then that I realized that the energy in my home was off somehow. Many times, emotional energies can be absorbed into a home and, because your home literally surrounds you, it can affect your mood.

Maybe the energy in your home feels off for some reason? Perhaps it feels stagnate or stifling in some way? Or possibly you just need to reset? You can use the ritual below after the banishing floor wash ritual found later in this book to bring positive energies and blessings into your home.

You will need

- A sachet (any light color will do)
- Lavender – to bring love, happiness, and peace
- Jasmine – to draw wealth, money and love
- Bay leaf – for protection
- Juniper – for love
- High John the Conqueror – for money, love, success, and happiness
- Frankincense incense – to lift the vibrations in the home

Procedure

1. Add all of the herbs and flowers to the sachet. Pour in the hot water. Let the infusion sit for a few minutes so the ingredients seep into the water.

2. Next, you'll bless the water by saying:

   By Earth, Air, Fire, and Water, I bless you!

3. Your floor wash is complete. Take the mixture and use it to wash down windows, walls, and the floors. Wash inward from your doorway to all corners of your home.

4. Chant:

   Bring peace, love, joy, and prosperity.
   All these things now come to me.

5. When you're finished, remove the sachet and discard the water.

6. Next, light the frankincense incense and walk throughout your home. As you walk, chant:

   Bring peace, love, joy, and prosperity,
   All these things now come to me.

Enjoy the feeling of peace and tranquility this ritual brings.

Ritual for Change and Transformation

A few years ago, I was living in New York a vibrant city that has everything; food festivals, music venues, movie events, concerts in the park, yoga in the park, Shakespeare in the park, museums, art galleries and, of course, parties: white parties, boat parties, garden parties, etc. Well, I was sick of it. I was done with the hustle and bustle of the city. I was pretty fed up and tired with that life in general. I was weary of the same old routine, day in and day out. I wanted to completely change my circumstances and life. I wanted to experience life in a new way. So, I crafted a ritual with Cerridwen. After performing this ritual, I started to consider making a big move. I began to investigate the idea of moving abroad. As I did so more and more information flowed to me about different avenues I could take to begin living abroad. Finally, about a month after performing this ritual I was contacted by a recruiter for a job in Japan! And I jumped at the chance. I can hear you asking now, "Isn't Cerridwen a white goddess. Who is she?" Remember we're using what works and stepping out of our comfort zones. I want you to be able to use any and all goddesses or powers.

Cerridwen is the goddess of transformation and rebirth in Welsh mythology. She's famous for her magical cauldron of transformation. In magic, the cauldron can symbolize rebirth and transformation, among other things. According to myth, she had a son who was so ugly, she feared no one would love him. To help him overcome his ugliness, she brewed a special potion in her magic cauldron. LOL!

This potion would make him the wisest person alive, but it had to be brewed for a full year and a day. It also required constant watching, so she had a servant boy monitor the potion. This servant boy accidentally dropped some of the potion on himself and gained the wisdom intended for her son.

A chase then ensued with both Cerridwen and the boy transforming into various animals including a hare, fish and birds. Eventually, the servant boy was caught and swallowed whole. However, the story doesn't end there. Cerridwen somehow became pregnant and gave birth to the servant boy himself and tossed him into a river. However, the boy survived and became the wisest man alive.

In this myth, we can see both Cerridwen's transformative powers and connection to rebirth. You can harness her powers to help transform your life.

You will need

- 1 white candle – for new beginnings
- 4 green candles – for growth
- Dried yellow daffodil – for luck
- Lavender essential oil – for happiness and peace
- Olive oil – for blessings
- Sage incense – for wisdom
- A plate

Procedure

1. Ground and center.

2. Cast a circle and call the four quarters.

3. Light the sage incense and keep it close by, so that the scent fills your work area.

4. Charge the white candle while setting the intention that this candle is for change and transformation.

5. With a pin, carve your name or your astrological symbol onto the white candle to symbolize yourself.

6. Anoint the candles with olive oil mixed with a couple of drops of lavender essential oil.

7. Dress the candles by rolling them in the dried daffodil leaves.

8. Place the white/yellow candle in the center of the plate (melt a bit of wax on the bottom to secure it) and surround it with the 4 green candles.

9. Light the candles and say:

   Goddess Cerridwen, I ask that you be here with me now. Help to trigger the change and transformation I seek in my life.

10. Meditate on the changes you desire and visualize your life as you intend it to be.

11. Say the following:

    Goddess Cerridwen, bless and guide me on my journey of transformation.

12. Let the candles burn down.

—Don't forget to leave an offering for any Spirit or GOD / GODESS Called to assist you in your work! ☺

Bring Peace to Your Workplace

I think we've all had at least one job that we hated. I know I did. For about a year, I worked in a small office with a toxic environment. Well, the biggest issue wasn't the cattiness, or backstabbing, or vaguely condescending attitude of my coworkers. No, the biggest problem was the lack of peace. Someone was always yelling or sniping at someone else. They didn't like me, but they could barely stand each other. As you can imagine, it wasn't a productive environment. I realized that I needed to calm these b@#$hes down. So I worked this spell, to great success. There were no more shouting matches or backbiting sessions in my immediate vicinity. The underlying current of resentment was replaced by the feeling of calm after a storm. This was perfect for me because I could finally focus on my work and... on finding a new job. This ritual may help you if you're currently facing a similar situation.

You will need

- ❀ Any pot for plants
- ❀ Tray to catch water
- ❀ Potting soil
- ❀ Peace lily bulb (any plant will do)
- ❀ Amethyst stones – for calm and peace
- ❀ 4 white votive candles – for peace and spirituality
- ❀ Water

Procedure

1. Ground and center.

2. Cast a circle and call the four quarters.

3. At your altar, place the pot on a flat surface. Next set the four candles around the pot.

4. Light the candles.

5. Sit in front of the plant and calm yourself. Think about what you want to happen. For example: "I want a peaceful workplace." Imagine how you'd feel if your workplace was drama-free. Feel the relief and the gratitude. Keep this thought and feeling firmly in mind as you go through the next steps.

6. Pour some of the potting soil into the pot to create a layer of dirt. Next, add the plant bulb and cover it with another layer of soil. Ensure that the bulb is completely covered. Now take the amethyst stones and bury them deep in the soil.

7. Pour water over the soil as you state the following:

   As you grow, so grows my peace.
   By Earth, Air, Water, and Fire.
   Heed me now, bring my desire.
   As I will it, so shall it be.

8. Pinch out the candles and take the plant to your workplace.

Place it somewhere near you, close your messy coworkers or somewhere with plenty of sunshine.

Angel Gabriel to Curb Overeating

I love food. Many of us do. Food is love. Food is comfort. It seems we're always eating; we eat when we're stressed, we eat when we're bored, we eat when we're happy, we eat when we're sad, and we eat to celebrate.

However, we know the downside of food obsession. The American obesity epidemic is severe and has spread across the pond with reports of growing numbers of obese and overweight people in the United Kingdom. And we know the downside for Black women, too. Obesity-related diseases such as diabetes, hypertension, heart disease, and stroke have plagued our community for too long.

But there's a ray of hope. Now more than ever I see Black women practicing health-consciousness. My friend Lisa attends a Zumba class religiously. Another friend, Jessica, has cut all sugar from her diet. Now that we have access to information about which exercises work best for each body type (I happen to be pear-shaped) and which diets work best for each body type (we're spoiled for choices such as paleo, low-carb, low-fat, no-fat, intermittent fasting), we have all the tools we need to make better choices. Here's a little spell that could help provide the boost you need on your journey to a healthier lifestyle:

Archangel Gabriel handles women's issues and helps with curbing bad habits. His color is silver, and he's directly linked to the powers of the moon. The moon is a powerful symbol for witches and women in particular. The moon is tied to water and our emotions. And it has been proven that emotional problems are often at the root of overeating. Therefore, we'll use the energies of the Angel Gabriel to stop overeating.

You will need

- White candle – for contact with angles
- Jasmine incense – linked with Gabriel
- Silver ring
- Bowl of water

Procedure

1. Ground and center.

2. Cast a circle and call the four quarters.

3. Light the candle and incense.

4. Hold the jewelry in your hand and say the following:

   Gabriel, Gabriel, Gabriel, archangel of the moon.
   I call to you, oh Gabriel, to clear away this gloom.

5. Dip your fingertips into the water and sprinkle it over the jewelry as you say:

   By your power, I bless this ring.
   In rightful hour to do its thing.
   Curb the ravenous beast in me.
   When I wear it, I will see:

That I can calm my hunger.
That I can set myself free!

Wear daily to encourage mindful eating and prevent over-eating.

Talisman for Courage to Ask for What You Want

Many people don't get what they want for one simple reason – they don't ask. I know many Black women with this problem. One particular instance stands out in my mind. I was on a cruise with Lisa, the friend I mentioned earlier. It was dinnertime and we were both starving. Now, if you've ever been on a cruise, you know that there's a ridiculous amount of food on offer. When you take a cruise, you should plan to gain at least 10 pounds. Anyhow, there were separate compartments at dinnertime, one housed a buffet and the other provided a seated dinner for a price.

Lisa and I had visited the buffet the night before and wanted to try the sit-down dinner. We arrived and were seated right away. Chatting as we looked over the menu, we each decided on a dish. I ordered the chicken entrée while Lisa opted to have the lamb entrée. As we waited for the food to arrive, many other travelers came to sit with us (it was a shared table). We didn't mind at all and just enjoyed the fascinating company. When our meals came out, the conversation slowed as everyone began to eat.

After a while, when we had finished about half of our meals and conversation started up again, I noticed that Lisa had an odd look on her face. I asked her if everything was alright and she said no, "They didn't bring the right meal, they brought chicken, but I asked for lamb." I looked at her plate and at her barely touched food and asked her why she didn't say anything. Her answer, "I didn't want to cause a problem."

Ladies, it isn't a problem to ask for what you want in life! In life, never accept chicken when you really want lamb! Use the spell below to help you find the courage to ask for what you want.

We'll be using Shango to empower the talisman. He's also known as Sango. He is an Orisha who epitomizes masculinity. He's the lord of thunder, war, drumming, dancing, fire, and male virility. He is also known to wield a double-headed ax.

You will need

- Thistle – for strength, to strengthen the spirit
- Yarrow – for courage
- Black cohosh – helps to strengthen courage in the meek
- Small agate stone – for strength, bravery, and courage
- Olive oil – to increase potency
- Bottle pendant with a cork

Procedure

1. Ground and center.

2. Cast a circle and call the four quarters.

3. Keeping your intent firmly in mind, add all herbs into the bottle. Add the agate stone. Finally, pour in enough oil to cover the herbs. Cover the bottle.

4. State the following:

   Shango, spirit of thunder and war, drumming, dancing, fire and male virility, come to me. Shango, wielder of the double-bladed ax, hear my plea. Shango, surrounded by fire, wearing red and white robes and with a crown on his head, be with me now. Shango, fill this talisman with your power. May it give me your courage and power. Whenever I wear this talisman, it will make me as courageous as you are. Shango, spirit of thunder, great and mighty warrior, wielder of the double-bladed ax, I thank you. Go in peace.

5. Leave the talisman on your altar for a few days. The talisman will help when you need the courage to speak your mind.

✬ Energy Elixir ✬

There are times on this long journey of witchcraft and living life as a wise-woman where your energy stores will be depleted. No matter how many vitamins you take or how dedicated you are to staying hydrated, you'll occasionally feel as if you're running on fumes. I know this has been the case for me. The responsibilities of work, social life, practicing the craft, and general wellness can be exhausting.

Maintain a healthy store of energy is paramount to life as a witch. I'll tell you a little story -a tale of a woman who liked to do too much at once. This woman wanted to write a spell book to help others, so she got to work. She started brainstorming, developing ideas, networking and gaining information, researching and investigating the needs of her intended audience. This woman started going through her BOS (Book of Shadows) pulling out spells, and outlining major points, checking and rechecking every minute detail of each spell. Finally, after having done all this; in addition to holding down a 9-5 job, maintaining a healthy lifestyle (as best she could), caring for a dog and for her love ones, she sat at her computer prepared to begin writing her first draft. She sat there, completely exhausted until she passed out with her head on the keyboard and a blank page mocking her. In the morning, with the page still blank, she reassured herself that she'd begin tomorrow, when she had more time and energy. That night, after performing her daily duties and reviewing her notes, she was ready to get down to business. Once again, her body failed her, and her unattained goals mocked her. That's ultimately when she realized her need and developed a recipe that got her up and going again.

Ladies obviously, I'm talking about me, but I could be talking about you, too. How many of you have goals in your life that you're gung ho about but can never seem to find the time *and* energy to accomplish? Low energy is a curse that will prevent you from maximizing your full potential. You need to energize and fuel yourself with enough sleep, enough water, with supplements and good sex (wink). Add this to the mix to give you the energy boost you need. Stop waiting for elusive 'energy' and create it!

You will need

- ⚜ Glass bottle
- ⚜ Glass bowl
- ⚜ Fresh spring water
- ⚜ Sparkling water
- ⚜ A Spoon (non-metal if you have it)
- ⚜ Dried Marigold leaves
- ⚜ A dash of lemon
- ⚜ Honey
- ⚜ Piece of orange agate

Timing

On a Sunday, just before noon

Procedure

1. Brew the tea by placing the flower into a tea cup and pouring hot water over the buds. Let this sit until it cools, and then strain the tea.

2. Next, take the tea and other items to your altar. Ground and center.

3. Call the four quarters.

4. Into the empty bottle add the tea, sparkling water, lemon juice and a few slices of lemon and 6 drops of honey.

5. Gently whirl the bottle in a clockwise motion six times and set it aside

6. Place the agate piece in the bowl and gently pour the spring water over it until it's completely submerged.

7. Place the bottle in the bowl of water so that it absorbs the energy of the crystal.

8. Say the following incantation:

    Spirits of fire, hear me. It's my will that you come to me and hear my desire. Fill, this with your energy; fill it with your power at this time in this hour.

9. Leave this mixture on your altar in the sun for at least six hours. It'll be charged by the energy of the sun and fire.

10. Store in a place where it'll catch sunlight.

11. Each day throughout the week, have a drink as you say the incantation.

    Spirits of fire, hear me. It's my will that you come to me and hear my desire. Fill me with your energy, fill me with you power at this time in this hour!

Chapter 3

Rituals for
Psychic Expansion

*Now I see, now I know
how to make my creations grow.*

ow I don't need to tell you that being a powerful witch means possessing psychic power because the two go hand in hand. However, the psychic power I'm referring to isn't the kind witnessed on the TV or in movies. No, I'm talking about something far more practical and integral to everyday life. I'm talking about the wellspring of personal inner power that stems from having a strong and steadfast inner world. I'm talking about the power that comes through when your spirit, mind, and body are in alignment. When this happens, you're able to focus yourself, your entire being on your intentions and then nothing can stop you. When you have this kind of alignment, you'll notice a natural expansion of your psychic awareness. Let the spells and rituals in this section help you in gaining that alignment, so the when you look at a mountain and say move, it moves, because all of yourself is in perfect accord with your desire.

Chakra Ritual

In my early twenties, I had trouble expressing my emotions. Whenever I needed to speak about my feelings, I'd feel my throat constrict and I would lose my breath. It happened every time. I could speak freely about any number of topics but when it came time to express my emotions, I just couldn't do it.

At the time I knew very little about chakras. I'd heard of the concept and that it was connected to mystical practices in India, but I viewed it as something we Westerners co-opted. We merged it with yoga workouts and packaged the concept for sale to the masses.

I've learned a lot since then. Thankfully, I now have a deeper understanding of chakras and the influence they have on behavior, emotions, and health. Once I began to meditate and work on my chakras (throat especially), I found it easier to express myself. I'm able to have better personal and professional relationships because I can freely talk about my feelings and set healthy boundaries.

There are seven chakras in the body. They go from the base of your spine to the top of your head. A blocked chakra could lead to a multitude of problems.

Let's examine them all:

The first chakra is the root chakra. It is located at the base of your spine. Its color is red and its element is earth. The seed sound for the element is LAM. It governs the physical, stability, and survival. When blocked, you may experience sluggishness, stress, or anxiety. You may even have financial problems, or you are always just getting by. You may feel worried about attacks or just basic survival.

The second chakra is the sacral chakra. It is located just below your navel. Its color is orange and its element is water. The seed sound for the element is VAM. When blocked, you may be constantly bored and may be afraid of change. Because it's linked to your sexuality, you may also experience sexual problems such as low sex drive, shame surrounding sex, or difficulty with sexual and emotional intimacy. You may also be prone to addictive behaviors.

The third chakra is the solar plexus chakra. It's located two inches above the navel. Its color is yellow and its element is fire. The seed sound is RAM. It governs the relationship you have with yourself, your sense of self-worth, and feelings about your personal power. When blocked, you may experience low self-confidence and other self-esteem problems.

The fourth chakra is the heart chakra. It's situated in the center of the chest above the heart. Its color is green and its element is air. The seed sound for the element is YAM. The heart chakra governs our feelings of love and compassion for ourselves and others. When blocked, you may have difficulty giving and receiving love or compassion. You may hold on to past hurts, finding it hard to trust or relate to others.

The fifth chakra is the throat chakra. It resides in the middle of the throat. Its color is blue and its element is ether. The seed sound for this element is HAM. The throat chakra governs communication and self-expression. When it's blocked, you may fear speaking up about your wants or feelings. You may feel like your voice isn't heard or doesn't matter.

The sixth chakra is the third eye chakra. It is located in the center of your forehead between your eyebrows. Its color is indigo and its element is light. The seed sound for this element is AUM. The third eye governs intuition, psychic abilities, and extrasensory perception. When blocked, you may have a feeling of pointlessness or struggle to find meaning in your life. You may also have trouble making decisions or have problems finding your path in life.

The seventh chakra is the crown chakra. It's found at the top of the head. Its color is violet and its element is thought, all senses, or consciousness. The seed sound for this element is OM. The crown chakra governs your spirituality and your connection to the cosmos or the divine. When blocked, you may exhibit a lack of connection to the universe.

This ritual will help to clear chakra blockages:

You will need

- ❀ Quartz crystal – to open yourself spiritually and psychically
- ❀ Any pleasant incense – to alter your mood

Procedure

1. Light the incense.

2. Lay down comfortably in a quiet place. Ensure that your back is straight. Place the quartz crystal on your forehead.

3. Take a few deep breaths to inhale. Chant the seed sound, LAM. As you do, imagine a glowing red ball at the base of your spine. As you continue to chant, imagine that glowing red ball turning into a swirling vortex of red energy.

4. Take another deep breath in and, as you exhale, envision a glowing orange light about two inches below your navel. Chant the seed sound, VAM. As you do, see that glowing orange ball begin to spin until it becomes a swirling vortex.

5. Take a deep breath again; and, as you exhale, sense a glowing yellow ball about two inches above your navel. Chant the seed sound, RAM. As you chant, see the glowing yellow ball begin to spin faster and faster until it becomes a swirling vortex.

6. Once again, take a deep breath in and, as you exhale, imagine a glowing green ball in the center of your chest. Chant the seed sound, YAM. As you chant, the glowing green ball begins to spin, turning into a swirling vortex.

7. Now breathe in deeply and, on your exhalation, imagine a glowing blue ball in the middle of your throat. Chant the seed sound, HAM. As you chant, concentrate on the glowing blue ball as it begins to spin faster and faster until it becomes a swirling vortex in your throat.

8. Again, take a deep breath in and, as you exhale, visualize a glowing indigo ball between your eyebrows. Chant the seed sound, AUM. As you chant, see the glowing ball begin to spin until it turns into a whirling vortex.

9. Take another deep breath in and, as you exhale, imagine a glowing violet light at the crown of your head. Chant the seed sound, OM. As you chant, picture the glowing violet light begin to spin faster and faster until it is a whirling vortex.

10. Take another deep breath in and, as you exhale, see a pure white light entering the crown of your head. See the white light pass through each swirling vortex of energy, connecting them, until it reaches the base of your spine. Take a final deep breath in and see yourself glowing brightly with that white light.

☆ Psychic Tea ☆

It's time for another true-life story. There was a time when I wanted a better apartment. I lived on the outskirts of a city, but my job was in the city center. My commute to work was an hour and a half each day! I had to wake up before 5:00 am just to make it to work on time. After a year of this crazy schedule, I was ready to move. I had two options: I could move immediately to the downtown area and pay an exorbitant rent for a tiny space, or I could undergo the long, arduous, and seemingly impossible search for the perfect apartment, in the right location and at the right price — in New York City. I had a self-imposed deadline in mind and wanted to move as quickly as possible. Finally, a choice came between two apartments.

The first option was close to my office and in my price range, but it was the size of a closet. The second choice was also closer to my office and had what I considered to be a livable space. However, the rent was higher than I could handle (I wanted to be able to eat). I had a week to decide, according to the rental agent.

I decided to turn to the tarot for a sign, so I brewed a cup of this tea and prepared to do my reading. However, as I sat sipping this tea and contemplating my options, a thought came to me in a flash: "Let them both go," it said. Well, I was irritated, but I always follow my flashes of intuition. So, I let them both go.

Three weeks later, an officemate announced that she was leaving the company and she was looking for someone to take over her lease. And that was how I got my great apartment in New York City. I think this tea can help when you need to contemplate any tricky problem.

You will need

- ❀ Peppermint – for psychic powers, also for sleep
- ❀ Dandelion Root – for divination
- ❀ Star anise – for psychic powers
- ❀ Dried orange peel – for divination

Procedure

1. Brew the tea by placing the herbs into a teacup.

2. Then slowly pour hot water into your cup while thinking of your intention for the tea.

3. Allow the herbs to infuse the water for 5-10 minutes. Then strain and enjoy.

4. Sit with this cup of tea; and as you enjoy the flavor, ponder a question, situation, or problem.

The tea will help you gain some much-needed insight. Alternatively, you could drink the tea before doing any psychic, divination, or astral travel work to enhance your psychic perception.

Mystical Tuning Meditation

Many times, we get bogged down in the mundane aspects of life. Many of us are only focused on finishing our to-do lists.

It's easy to forget how truly mystical the world is when there is so much to be done. You have to cook breakfast for the kids, take them to school, go to work, pick *up* the kids, then make dinner and help them with their homework. It never ends and sometimes it feels like you might drown under the flood of responsibilities. When you need a break from hustle and bustle of reality, take a moment and perform this meditation.

You will need

- ❀ Any incense
- ❀ Quartz crystal, if you have it

Procedure

1. Light your incense and allow the fumes to fill the space.

2. Hold your quartz crystal firmly in your hand. Sit comfortably in a quiet place, back straight and with your feet firmly planted on the floor. Begin by taking in three deep breaths to relax.

3. Breathe in deeply and as you do see your stomach expanding. Then exhale slowly through your nose. Continue to breathe this way.

4. With your eyes closed, recall a happy memory of yourself as a child. See your location, surroundings, and everything around you. And breathe.

5. Think of a happy memory from five years later. Remember it as vividly and in as much detail as possible.

Remember where you were, the clothes you were wearing, what you were doing and with whom. And breathe deeply.

6. Keep doing this: vividly remembering a happy memory in five-year intervals until you reach your current age.

7. Now, see all of your past selves lined up one after the other, with each version surrounded by the vivid pictures of your memories, almost like a picture book.

8. Imagine all of these past selves looking at current you with smiling encouragement and approval. Each self holds a glowing green orb of energy in their hands. This green energy is one of the purest love.

9. Envision them reaching out a hand towards your current self; and as they touch you, you become filled with that loving, supporting energy. See and feel it traveling through your body filling you up so much that the green energy begins radiating outward.

10. See and feel yourself so filled with the green light of self-love that every breath exudes this glowing green energy. It surrounds and cocoons you. Each breath you take expels more of the love energy until it encompasses all that surrounds you.

11. Know that all events past and present, all versions of yourself, your current setting - are all connected by this loving energy.

12. Breathe in with the understanding that this is the true magic of the universe. And breathe out knowing that you're at the center of it.

Isis to Increase Magical Power

One of the first spells I ever performed was a spell to increase my magical power. But before I could perform the spell, I had to get over one major hitch: to become comfortable with wanting to be powerful. It seemed like common sense. If I wanted quicker, more powerful results, I should try spells to amplify my personal power. However, the desire for power and my shame about wanting it resulted in me dropping the idea altogether.

I wasn't comfortable with power. I was apprehensive with admitting that I desired power. I often felt powerless and refused to use or even see my own power. Likewise, I think many Black women may be able to relate. I was raised in the church, like many Black women. And the Black church interprets the Bible in a specific way. The Black church's interpretation makes the desire for riches (which are usually linked to power) seem dishonorable.

The quotes below display this mindset:

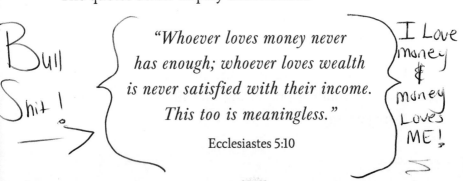

Bull
Shit !

"Whoever loves money never has enough; whoever loves wealth is never satisfied with their income. This too is meaningless."

Ecclesiastes 5:10

I Love money & money Loves ME!

"Better the little that the righteous have
than the wealth of many wicked; for the power
of the wicked will be broken, but the
LORD upholds the righteous. "

Psalm 37: 16-17

Also, in my mind power meant "possession or control, authority, or influence over others" ("Power," Merriam-Webster, 2019), which just didn't sit right with me. Desiring to control others seemed morally wrong. But when I began to think of power as "the ability to act or produce an effect" and as "a source or means of supplying energy" ("Power", Merriam-Webster, 2019), I started to accept that having power was an asset.

Moreover, I avoided power because I often felt wronged by those who had power over me. I saw all authority figures as slave drivers and overseers. I thought they were put in place to oppress me. When I thought of "power," I envisioned the corporate executives or corrupt politicians who always seem to get away with murder. When I reflected on "power," I pictured every middle management boss who demanded your best, gave little in return, and was quick to throw you under the bus. And when I considered "power," I imagined every elder in the community who thought they were due my respect because of their advanced age, regardless of their behaviors. LOL!

Obviously, I had a problem with authority. I had to grow up and escape the victim mentality. I had to shake off the feeling that "the man" was trying to oppress me. I had to let go of the childish need to buck convention just for the sake of being a contrarian. Finally, I had to learn to acknowledge and embrace my own power. I realized I had power and having more of it was advantageous. Ladies, you have power and should strive to acquire more power. And the goddess Isis can help you get it.

Who's Isis? You may have heard of her. She's the Egyptian goddess of motherhood, fertility, and magical power. The story of Isis bringing her husband Osiris back from the dead is well known. But we're tapping into her power because of another myth.

This myth tells how Isis gained magical power through cunning and craftiness. She set a poisonous snake on the god Ra. Ra was the god of the sun and extremely powerful. In fact, he originally had all the magical power. However, he was bitten by the poisonous snake and needed someone to cure him. Isis stepped in and volunteered for the job on one condition — that Ra tell her his true name. Without any other choice, Ra agreed and he revealed his true name in return for the cure. Because she knew Ra's true name, Isis had power over him and thereby gained his magical power.

You can call on Isis to help increase your magical power.

You will need

- The High Priestess tarot card – imagination, feminine power, spirituality
- The Empress tarot card – creativity, feminine power, fertility
- Silver candle – the color associated with Isis
- Bowl

❀ Milk

❀ Honey

❀ Myrrh incense – associated with Isis

Timing

On a Monday, waxing moon, moon in Libra, Virgo, Cancer, Taurus, Scorpio or Sagittarius

Procedure

1. Ground and center.

2. Cast a circle and call the four quarters.

3. Anoint the silver candle with oil and dress it with herbs. As you do this step, focus on Isis. Think of her desire for Ra's power. Think of the cunning she used to acquire it. Think of how you now desire power. Know that Isis will assist you because she understands the desire for power.

4. Light the candle and incense. Look at the High Priestess tarot card. Study the picture and examine every symbol carefully. Know that it represents feminine power, spirituality, and imagination. Recognize that it's your intent to increase these attributes in yourself. Place the card in front of the candle.

5. Look at the Empress tarot card. Study the picture and examine every symbol carefully. Know that it represents creativity, feminine power, and fertility. Recognize that it's your intent to increase these attributes

within yourself. Lay the card in front of the candle beside the High Priestess tarot card.

6. Now gaze into the flame and speak these words:

Isis Goddess of magic and healing, daughter of Geb and Nu, wife of Osiris and mother of Horus. Great Goddess Isis, the Divine One, Lady of the Words of Power, be with me here in this moment. I seek your audience. Great Isis, the Divine One, be here with me in this moment.

Isis, who used cunning and power to trick the great god Ra into revealing his true name. In doing so, you acquired great magical power. Isis, Great Lady of magic. I seek your assistance. Increase my magical power. Increase it now, so that I grow in power as you did. As this candle burns, my magical power will grow! Please accept this offering in gratitude.

7. Pour the milk into the bowl and a good amount of honey. Then state:

Isis, Goddess of magic and healing, daughter of Geb and Nu, wife of Osiris and mother of Horus. Great Goddess Isis, the Divine One, Lady of the Words of Power, I thank you for your assistance. Go in peace.

8. Allow the candle to burn down completely. Leave the offering out for a day, then dispose of it.

Altar Setup to Connect
with Spiritual Forces

Years ago, I began noticing little pinpricks of light that would quickly flash in front of my eyes. At first, I worried that I had some illness that made me see these things. It was upsetting because that was the last thing I needed. See, I was going through a tough time in my life at that point. I had a "good job" in New York with a reputable firm, but I was miserable.

The environment was draining, and my boss was the worst: she was a little white woman with blond hair who dressed like Murphy Brown (I didn't know they still made clothes like that). Anyway, this woman would yell and go into little fits. She'd also rake her hands through her hair and shake it when she was annoyed. The department consisted of women only (often the case in marketing) and one male part-time intern. These were all older women who lived in Long Island and commuted to the city every day. Because of internal rivalries, the environment was toxic.

I needed guidance: should I stay at the "good job" or try my luck elsewhere in a not so great economy? Luckily, I mentioned the pinpricks to a good friend, who told me to relax. "It's probably just your guardian angel," she said. That's when inspiration hit, and I got the idea to contact my guardian angels for a little wisdom.

I created an altar to connect with them. I asked for assistance and was led to the truth. I didn't need that job, the job needed me. So, with that firmly in mind, I set out to find a new job. Within the first week, I received numerous callbacks. Three weeks later, I landed a new, better position. Ever since, my angel altar has been a fixture in my home.

That's not all. Three years later, my previous boss applied and interviewed with my current employer. My supervisor came to me and asked if she was a good person to hire. I won't tell you what I said, but I'm sure you can guess.

Anyhow, many of us need guidance and seek to connect to the other side for help. Maybe you want to connect with an ancestor or a relative who passed away? Or perhaps you feel called to a particular entity, god, goddess, angel, elemental, or spirit? Setting up an altar is a great way to bring that energy into your life.

You will need

- An empty bowl
- 2 large white candles – for spiritual connection
- Lavender essential oil – angel scent
- Dried roses – for psychic powers
- Dried jasmine – angel scent
- Olive oil – for blessings and purification
- Rose incense – for love and psychic powers
- Small tray of crystals – to charge the space
- Angel statue – to represent the angel
- Item representing the entity (I used a feather)
- Bouquet of dried or artificial flowers – for decoration

Procedure

1. Ground and center.

2. Cast a circle and call the four quarters.

3. In a mortar, grind the dried ingredients.

4. In a small bowl, mix about an ounce of olive oil and 4 drops of essential oil.

5. Dress the candles with the olive oil mixture and roll the candles in the dried flowers.

6. Purify yourself by dipping your finger in the olive oil, anointing your forehead, and saying: 'I purify myself to enter this sacred space.'"

7. Sage and purify the area you intend to use as your altar.

8. Create a sacred space by saying the following:

   By the power of air, I bless you.
   By the power of fire, I bless you.
   By the power of water, I bless you.
   By the power of air, I bless you!

9. Place the statue in the center of the area. Lay the bouquet of flowers behind and around the statue.

10. Charge the tray of crystals with loving intent and set it in front of the statue.

11. Position the candles on either side of the statue.

12. Lay the feather to the right of the statue.

13. Finally, light the candles.

14. Send up a small prayer to your spirit to let them know that this is the spirit's sacred space.

15. Stand in front of the altar and commune with the spirits. Let them know that you wish to feel their presence, that you want them to enter this sacred space. Talk to them and ask them questions.

16. When you're ready, thank them and close the circle.

Please note that this procedure can be used to set up an altar to any spirit or deity. Simply substitute in the items that correspond to the deity of your choice.

To Induce Vivid Dreams

If you want a glimpse of the future, this ritual could help. For a long time, I was resistant to divination. I didn't like doing tarot readings or consulting runes. I thought that by receiving troubling news, I'd subconsciously draw that future to me. After some consideration, I realized that I was letting fear prevent me from having an exciting mystical experience.

So, I dove into divination and, along the way, I began to love the experience. I finally understood what many other witches already knew: that you're only glimpsing a possible future and, by knowing what could happen, you can change your path. After that little epiphany, I longed to experience more and go deeper. Once I became open to that type of psychic phenomenon, my dreams became more vivid. It opened up my awareness and caused me to seek out prophetic dreams.

If you're open to having a similar experience, try the ritual below:

You will need

- Jasmine incense – for prophetic dreams and beautiful scent
- Marigold – for prophetic dreams and psychic powers
- Mimosa – for prophetic dreams
- Mugwort – for prophetic dreams and psychic powers
- Moonstone or clear quartz crystal
- Sachet

Procedure

Perform this ritual just before going to bed.

1. Place all of the items into the sachet. Light the incense and place the sachet over the smoke to charge it with your intent. Ask the smoke to aid you in receiving helpful visions.

2. Draw a bath with warm water and place the sachet inside. The bath should be taken in complete darkness.

3. Allow the energies to seep into the water. Then slip into the water yourself.

4. Now think of your problem or situation. You're not actively trying to find a solution. You are just meditating on the issue. After 15-20 minutes, step out of the bath. Do not towel off, just allow the water to dry on your skin.

5. Take the sachet out and squeeze to remove the excess water.

6. Finally, place the sachet under your pillow as you speak the following:

    I seek an answer to my problem (think of the problem)

    Tonight, I place this under my pillow. In the dark of the night, I ask that the answers come to me in my dreams.

7. Place under your pillow each night until you receive guidance about the problem.

Chapter 4

Dealing with Foes and Unwanted Energies

> *My inner strength allows me to bend but never break.*

I hate that we as Black women have to deal with certain situations in life. The list of bullshit we have to face daily seems endless. On the regular we have to muddle through any one of the following irritation inducing circumstances or events; a nosy gossip, a cheating spouse, a backstabbing friend, a psychic vampire, leaches, broken romance or internal criticism. Many of these situations stem from our own actions. However, others are beyond our control and are just a natural consequence of billions of people living on a planet with (supposedly) limited resources. These situations can have detrimental effects on our mental and emotional wellbeing. And you know that being a successful witch depends largely on your internal condition. You need some solutions, and below are some wonderful ideas for how to handle the problematic situations we often find ourselves encountering.

Bind Someone

I have an aunt who gets on my last nerve. I love her dearly, but she's the family gossip. She's truly the auntie who's always in everyone's business. She's forever meddling or spreading rumors and presenting them as truth. I endured her antics throughout my entire childhood without much complaint. But after she blabbed about troubles with a boyfriend (he was unemployed at the time) to the entire family at Sunday dinner, I decided to do something about it.

However, a curse was out of the question. Because I loved her, I didn't want to hurt her. I just wanted her to stop gossiping about me, so. I created this ritual.

It's great to use if someone is causing trouble in your life and for whatever reason, you don't want to hex or curse him or her. For example, a family member or friend may be doing something disruptive and you want the person to stop that troublesome behavior.

You will need

- One white candle – not black because you don't want to cause harm

⊛ Knotweed – for binding woes and miseries

⊛ Olive oil – for potency

⊛ A long white ribbon – to bind

⊛ Picture of the person

Procedure

1. Ground and center.

2. Cast a circle and call the four quarters.

3. Engrave the candle with the target's name. Dress the candle with the oil and knotweed.

4. Place the picture under the candle.

5. Light the candle. Focus on the flame for 15-20 minutes and think of the destructive behavior you want stopped.

6. Let the candle burn down completely. Don't let the picture burn. Remove it when the candle has almost burnt out. Afterward, collect the wax and wrap the picture around it.

7. Take one end of the long ribbon and begin to wrap the picture and wax.

8. As you wrap the ribbon around, chant the following:

In the name of Adonai, I bind you (name of person)
(3 times)

In the name of Elohim, I bind you (name of person)
(3 times)
In the name of EL Shadai, I bind you (name of person)
(3 times)
I bind you!
I bind you!
I bind you!

9. Bury the bundle in a safe place.

Witch Bottle to Silence a B#*&h

Some b#*&h has been talking smack about you and bad-mouthing you behind your back. Maybe she's a colleague at work or perhaps a jealous family member or an ex-friend who's spilling all your secrets? You may think to yourself, "I don't care what's said about me, I know it's not true!" That may be an admirable attitude to have. But if the slander continues, it could be detrimental to you.

I worked with a woman named Zelda. Zelda was a quiet woman who didn't stand out much. She kept her head down and powered through her work day by day. During the busy season, management decided that the department need extra help. So, they hired a temp, Janet.

Janet was younger than Zelda and had less experience, but Janet was crafty. Janet started to go over Zelda's work quietly, looking for mistakes. And if she found anything, she'd go straight to the supervisor. Together they would badmouth Zelda behind her back. Pretty soon the entire office got into it, and Zelda became public enemy number one in the department. She had a huge red target painted on her back.

It wasn't long before Zelda left due to the stress she faced on the job. And Janet, the temp, was hired for a full-time permanent position.

So, you see, ladies, you should always take slander seriously. It's a direct attack on your reputation. And your reputation is all you have. Use this when someone is trying to damage your reputation.

You will need

- A medium glass jar with a cover
- A black candle – to fight evil
- Cloves – to stop others from gossiping about you
- Slippery elm – halts gossip
- Bay leaf – for protection
- Rice – for protection
- Ginger root, sliced – for power
- Obsidian stones – hex breaking
- Dragon's blood incense – for potency

Procedure

1. Ground and center.

2. Cast a circle and call the four quarters.

3. Take the black candle in hand and write the name of the person you wish to silence with a pin or needle.

4. Light your incense and hold the bottle over it letting the smoke fill the bottle.

5. Light the candle and place it in the center of the glass jar. Melt some wax on the bottom, so it'll stand.

6. As the candle burns, think of the person who's bad-mouthing you or spilling your secrets. Imagine his or her mouth being sewn shut. See this person struggling to open one's mouth but being unable to. Imagine the panic in their eyes. Feel the satisfaction of having silenced your enemy. Once you have done this for about 15-20 minutes, pinch out the candle. Do this for 3 nights and on the final night allow the candle to burn down completely.

7. Add the slippery elm, cloves, and obsidian stones over the wax. Next, layer on the ginger root, then the bay leaf. Finally, pour in the rice and cover the jar. Feel the satisfaction of having silenced your foe for good.

Keep the bottle somewhere safe.

Punish an Enemy

So, someone has dared to cross you and you want RE-VENGE! Now, I know that many books on magic shy away from offering these types of spells. But I acknowledge that there will come a time in a witch's life where she'll have to "correct" someone. It happened to me; there was a time when I required this spell. This is another work-related story so buckle in, ladies.

During my last year in college, I was lucky enough to land a great internship in my field with one of the most prestigious firms in my industry. The internship was more of a rotational training program where students spent three months in each of the different departments. During the first three months, I worked alongside many dedicated professionals. In that first department, everyone got along splendidly.

Unfortunately, when it came time to move on to my next three-month rotation, I faced the biggest roadblock of my burgeoning career. And surprise! It was another Black woman. As an aside: Ladies, there are too many of us who do this. Too many of us try to sabotage each other. What happened to sisterhood?

Anyhow, this Black woman liked to put on a front of being jovial and helpful. She loved to play into the big momma role with Black people. She liked dispensing down-home wisdom, cracking judgmental jokes (a lot of people hide their malice behind a mask of humor), and generally being a "guiding hand" for us.

It became apparent to me right away that she had some unresolved issues. She sought to "take care" of others under a guise of selflessness, but she was really a psychic vampire who experienced highs by feeding on the attention of others. She thrived on being needed and flaunting her expertise. And she loved to tell people what they should do to solve their "problems."

If you didn't take her advice or pay attention to her when she performed her antics, she'd become angry and lash out aggressively. One night at happy hour, everything came to a head. She walked into the bar and ordered four drinks for herself. I knew then that she was ready to perform. It was still a bit early for me, so I had a soda. She downed the drinks one after the other. She was loud and sloppy throughout the night. She got angry with me when I refused to take shots and get sloppy, too.

She thrived on the attention, you see. And in this case, she desperately needed the attention. She became angry when I talked to any man at the bar that she hadn't okayed. She was infuriated whenever I turned away from her big show. I realized that she was pissed any time she wasn't the focus of my attention.

Finally, I left because I'd had enough. The next day at work, she gave me the silent treatment. It wasn't long before that rotational supervisor suddenly became cold toward me. I was given some of the worst assignments. My dream internship became a nightmare and I was concerned that she'd do something that would cause me to be booted from the program. I was also pissed off at her. Nothing infuriates me more than someone trying to mess with my career or my money.

So, I called on Set to rain down fiery fury on her. And that week she suffered an unfortunate accident: she somehow twisted her knee on a night out. She couldn't be in the office for a week. And one week later my rotation with that department ended, and I moved onto a different department.

Set came through for me and could assist you, too. But who's Set? He's the Egyptian god of the desert, storms, darkness, and chaos. He is brother to Osiris and Isis. In one myth, he kills his brother out of jealousy. Because of this, Set has a bad reputation. However, I must say that he's a powerful deity to have on your side.

Just a brief warning – don't use this on people who haven't wronged you personally.

You will need

- 4 red candles – to channel your anger and malice
- 1 black candle – to represent your enemy
- Picture of the enemy

Timing

On a Tuesday or Saturday, during a waning moon

Procedure

1. Ground and center.

2. Cast a circle and call the four quarters.

3. Carve the name of your enemy onto the black candle.

4. Put the black candle on top of the picture of your target.

5. Next, take the red candles and write out words of ill will that you want to happen to your target. Carve words such as disaster, malice, despair, trouble, calamity, misfortune, poverty, etc. Think of how the person wronged you and of how much you want him or her to

suffer and pour all of that energy into the candles. Throughout this spell keep the feeling of anger for your enemy.

6. Surround the black candle with the four red ones and light them all.

7. Once again, let your hatred and malice rise within you, and then speak these words:

Set, god of the desert and storms.
Set, god of the darkness and chaos.
I call to you, oh mighty Set,
Set, who slew his brother Osiris.
Set, god of storms, disorder, and violence, I call to you.
Hear me now. Bring your wrath upon my enemy (name of person).
Let them see to not f#*k with me!
Punish (name of person) for what he or she has done.
Let (name of person) feel your power
Set, god of the desert and chaos, I thank you.
Go in peace.

8. Allow the harmful feelings to leave you. Feel certain that your enemy has been punished.

9. Let the candles burn down and toss away the remaining wax.

Read Later!

Banishing Floor Wash Ritual

One summer, I decided to have a little rooftop cookout with a couple of family members. I intended it to be small; just my sister, a couple of cousins, and a couple of friends. However, someone invited someone else, and suddenly I had a raging party on my hands.

Maybe something similar has happened to you? You initially intended to have a small gathering, but someone let it slip. Perhaps it was your husband or your kid who's still learning when to keep one's mouth shut? Possibly your best friend accidentally (on purpose) let others know? Once the secret was out, the small gathering turned into a big frat party. Your siblings brought their friends and/or significant others. Your best friend dragged along her new man. And to make matters worse, she also invited that *other* friend you don't really like. As a witch, you know that uninvited or unwanted guests often bring unwanted energies with them.

Well, a banishing floor wash is the perfect way to deal with that mess. The ritual below is perfect to rid your home of unwanted energies. You should use the ritual in combination with the previous blessing ritual. Once you're done, your home will radiate a high vibrational frequency of love, peace, and comfort.

You will need

- Ammonia – for purifying and cleansing
- St. John's wort – to banish negative energies
- Bay leaf – for purification

- ❀ Salt – for purification
- ❀ White sage incense – to drive away malevolent forces

Procedure

1. Add the ingredients to warm water and then bless it by saying:

   By the power of Air, I bless you.
   By the power of Fire, I bless you.
   By the power of Water, I bless you.
   By the power of Earth, I bless you.

2. Take the mixture and wash your floors working from top to bottom; from inside out toward the doorway (wash the walls too!) while chanting the following:

   Banish the negative,
   Banish the old,
   Leave only positive,
   Leave only gold!

3. After you're done, allow the floor to dry completely and throw out the water (down the toilet is fine).

4. Next, charge the incense with the intention to clear out negativity. Light the incense and walk through your home as you chant the following:

   By Earth, Air, Fire, and Water I purify this space.

Allow the smoke to fill your entire home. Then let the incense burn down.

Banishing Powder

There may be times when you're simply too tired, lazy or pressed for time to perform a complete floor wash ritual. However, the need rid your home of negative energies doesn't just disappear. In that case a floor sweep may be the answer to the problem. This banishing powder is the perfect solution for those days when you're looking to have a little quickie and get things back on track.

You will need

- Cloves – to drive away hostile and negative forces
- Bay leaves – to ward off negativity and evil
- Mint – to rid a place of evil
- St John's Wort – for protection and to ward of melancholy
- Mortar and pestle or coffee grinder

Procedure

1. Ground and center.

2. Cast circle and call the four quarters.

3. Simply grind herbs together into a fine powder while focused on your intent for the powder.

4. Place in an airtight container.

This powder can be used a floor sweep by sprinkling it in the corners of the home. Let it sit for 10 -15 minutes. Then the sweep up/ out of your home while envisioning all negative forces being cleared away. You can, of course use, this in ritual or add it to a candle; which I do below:

Banishing Candle

You will need

- Banishing powder
- Paraffin wax chips (1 pound will make four 6 oz. candles)
- Wicks
- Wick sticky tabs (available in craft stores)
- Pot
- Heat-resistant container (Pyrex measuring cup will do)
- Wooden stick
- 3-4 25ml glass containers with covers

Procedure

1. Secure the wick to the center of the candle mold or glass container using the wick sticky tabs.

2. Fill the pot halfway with water. Slowly heat the water (don't let it boil). Then carefully place the pyrex cup with the wax chips into the water. Allow the wax to

melt slowly. Once the wax is completely melted, re-move the pot from the stove.

3. Slowly pour the wax into glass jars. Now add the banishing powder from above. Stir in slowly using the wooden stick.

4. Roll the wick around the wooden stick to keep it in place as the wax sets. Leave the candle in a cool dry place for 24 hours.

I often use this on a Saturday and simply allow it to burn for a half hour or so. Sometimes I may also use it in the banishing ritual below:

Candle Ritual to Banish Self-Sabotaging Thought-forms

Why don't things last in my life? That was a question that I constantly asked myself in the past. I'm sure that some of you have asked this question at least once before. Why is it that the good things, which were attained with much struggle and difficulty, never seem to last for very long? I recall a few instances of struggling, clawing and grasping to achieve a long-held desire, only to attain it and watch it slip through my fingers. I'd revel in the high feeling of 'I've finally made it' and 'the struggle is over now'. Only for the situation to come tumbling back down again after a short time. It took some soul searching to get to the bottom of the situation, but I was able to see it for what it was. The problem, ladies, was self-sabotage. More specifically, it was self-sabotaging thought forms. What's a thought-form? Well, a thought-form is a thought that's repeated so often, with so much emotion behind it that it essentially takes on a life of its own. Think, "I'm worthless" enough times and with enough emotion and the thought will eventually become a living entity that will go out and work to bring about the corresponding reality. Thought-forms could be something you've created or be something that was said to you. Yes, other people's thoughts, ideas or wishes can become thought-forms that can affect you as well.

Quick story - I grew up fat. Well, I grew up plump as a kid, which then turned into being thick in my teens, which led to being plain obese as a young adult. Needless to say, I had much insecurity that stemmed from this issue. That's because contrary to current popular belief, being a Black female and being fat weren't accepted. It wasn't normal. This was before the fruits of decades of the American diet began to show up across the nation, especially in Black communities. As such the girls and women were expected to be thin, ideally. In fact, I could count the number of fat Black girls, children, and women on one hand. Being that size at that time was a literal hell for me. Could you imagine the thought forms circling around and bombarding me from within and without?

Anyone and everyone thought they could say and do whatever they liked to me and I had few allies, even in my family. My family members were often the main perpetrators of the emotional and physical traumas I suffered. I'm sure they didn't do most of it on purpose, but it still hurt and left lasting wounds.

Anyway, in my late teens early twenties, I went on a campaign to lose the excess weight. Miraculously, within a year, I dropped three dress sizes! Everyone was very impressed. However, I wasn't satisfied. I was determined to never be called or be looked at as fat again. So I went harder and dropped more weight until I was finally my ideal body weight. Unfortunately for me, I didn't think it was enough. Before long, the negative thoughts and self-criticism gained full control of the situation.

I was subject to a host of conflicting feelings about myself and my weight. Some stemming from within, others based on things people said to me. Feelings like, "I'll never be thin enough, I've always been fat and always will be; if I'm not careful I'm just going to gain all of the weight back because I didn't lose it in the 'right way.'" The main thought-form was, 'I'm so fat, and I'll never be good enough.'

Needless to say, I gained some weight back almost immediately after I attained the goal. But with all of the conflicted feelings and thought-forms that surrounded me and muddled my intentions, was it any wonder that was the reality I attracted?

All of this is to reiterate that if you find yourself in the same situation where your goals manifest but don't remain for very long, despite you best efforts, then you may need to take some action to clear away the thought-forms that may be bringing you down at that point.

You will need

- One banishing candle or black candle

- Parchment paper
- Pen
- Banishing powder
- Scissors
- Tweezers
- Fire-proof vessel

Timing

During the dark of the moon, Saturday, or Tuesday

Procedure

1. Ground and Center.

2. Cast a circle and call the four quarters.

3. Take a moment while in the circle to think of all the problematic and self-sabotaging thought-forms that are operating in your life. You can even ask the Universe to reveal them to you. Once you have an idea, begin to list them out on the parchment paper. I usually end up with a list of ten or more

4. Next, cut the parchment into strips separating each item on the list.

5. Light the candle and gazing into the flame say the following:

Spirits of Earth, spirits or Fire, spirits of Air, and spirits of Water, I call to you to witness and aid in this ritual. Banish all thought forms that no longer serve me.

6. Then, using the tweezers so that you don't burn your fingers, pick up the first slip of paper and touch it to the fire as you say the following:

By the power of Earth, Air, Fire and Water, I banish [fill in with petition] from my life. I send it back to the void from where it came, never to return.

7. Place the strip of paper in the fire-proof vessel and allow it to burn to ashes.

8. Repeat this process until you have burnt all the slips of paper.

9. Once finished, add the banishing powder or salt to the ashes and declare:

As I will it, so let it be!

10. Pinch out the candle flame.

11. Throw the ashes out or flush them down the toilet.

A note of warning: you may experience a bit of a headache while performing this ritual as you burn and banish. If you do, then feel free to stop where you are and leave the others slips of paper for another time. It may be tempting to try to rid yourself of every problem all at once but it's highly recommended that you pace yourself when doing this type of self-work.

Also, please note that this ritual is one that I recommend you perform regularly, whether once a week or once a month, to gain the greatest benefit. We're constantly bombarded with thoughts and ideas subconsciously and old ones sometimes resurface because of triggers. So, maintaining a weekly ritual to rid yourself of detrimental thought-forms may facilitate your progress.

Chapter 5

Love Spells

*I receive all the good things
I've called into my life.*

*T*ruly believe that everyone deserves love. And Black
women definitely deserve love, romance, and commitment if that's what they're truly seeking. However, too many of us are going without this important part
of life. I hate to break it to you, ladies: you may be able to do
it all on your own, but you shouldn't have to do so. Women
need support and emotional connections. Love energizes
and enlivens us. It wakes you up from your routine life and
sparks new awareness. In this section, you'll find solutions
for many of your amorous needs; from attracting a new lover

to drawing a partner, forging new friendships, and even ending a romance.

Spell to Draw a New Lover

I could have listed this spell in the wellbeing section because sexual satisfaction is self-care, too. However, I'm going to stick it here in the love spell section. Ladies, let's be real: sometimes you just need a man/or woman, to do what men do.

I think many Black women forget this. How often has this happened to you? You've been busy hustling and grinding, being a boss b!#*h, the CEO of You Inc. You're making strides up that corporate ladder or toward other goals. One day you look up (literally) and realize, "I haven't had sex in months!" How did this happen?

Well, now that you've noticed, you know that something must be done to remedy the situation. So, you sit down to look at your prospects and...it doesn't look good. The men in your immediate vicinity are all either unappealing physically, unstable mentally (you think), morally reprehensible, or spiritually unaware.

Being your witchy self, you know and understand that safe sex (it should always be safe!), has consequences. Sex is an exchange of energies and, because of this, you're not going to accept any ole' body. You have standards and needs to ensure will be satisfied.

I must say that this very situation has happened to me. I was between boyfriends and still recovering from a bad breakup. To hold back the pain, I threw myself into work, side projects, friends, family, and social events. When I noticed how long it had been, I took matters into my own hands. Within two weeks, I had several choices present themselves to me. And I indulged and reveled in the results!

Well, try this little spell and you may be pleasantly surprised with the outcomes...

You will need

- Red male and female candles
- Olive Oil – for potency
- Cardamom – for lust and love
- Cinnamon – for lust
- Galangal – to promote lust
- Ginseng – for male sexual potency
- Juniper – to bring good luck in sexual relations
- Dragon's blood incense – for potency
- The lover's tarot card

Timing

On a Friday, during a waxing moon

Procedure

1. Ground and center.

2. Cast a circle and call the four quarters.

3. In a mortar, crush all the herbs together.

4. Anoint the candles with olive oil as you think of your need.

5. Cover the candles with the mixture.

6. Place the two candles on your altar facing each other. Put the lover's tarot card in front of the candles.

7. Light the incense and light the candles.

8. Staring into the flames think of your need. Then imagine your ideal lover satisfying your sexual desires. Think of all you'd do with this person. Feel the arousal building within you.

9. Chant the following:

   It's a lover I seek;
   Strong and powerful and never meek.
   His passion I'll inflame,
   And for me he'll do the same.
   Draw him now to me,
   As I will it, so shall it be!

10. Now feel as though you've already received the sexual gratification as you gaze into the flames. Finally, after 15 minutes, pinch out the candles.

Work this spell for 3 days. On the final day, let the candles burn down completely. Discard the remaining wax.

End a Romance

Okay, you've had your fun and now you're tired of your lover. Or maybe the love has dried up, but your lives are so entangled that it may not be easy to walk away? Things can get very messy when you try to end a romantic relationship.

A male friend of mine named David had this exact problem. He'd been in a relationship with his girlfriend for two years. When they first met, he thought she was spectacular and that he'd hit the jackpot. She was smart, sexy, and able to hold a conversation for more than a minute. Their connection progressed quickly, so within a year, they moved into a rental home together, brought a car, adopted a dog, and got engaged.

However, within a year of moving in together, the relationship began to sour. She was controlling, manipulative, and overly dramatic. By the end of the second year, he'd had enough. But it was hell to untangle his life from hers, and the whole situation became a nightmare of harassing phone calls, temper tantrums, and court proceedings.

Don't be like David. Try the spell below when it's time to end a relationship and you wish to do so gracefully and without drama.

You will need

- A black male candle – to represent the male, black for banishing

⊛ Power to destroy talisman – to break up or end a situation. The black and white picture can be printed from the internet.

Procedure

1. Ground and center.

2. Cast a circle and call the four quarters.

3. Carve the target's name on the candle.

4. Fold the power to destroy talisman away from yourself as you the following:

Now our love is done,
The time has come.
To see him off forever.
This is the end of our endeavor.
Release him now, send him away,
So that new love will come, so that new love can stay!

5. Place the talisman under the candle.

Burn the candle for three days while imaging the peaceful dissolution of the relationship.

Attraction in Action Sachet

This talisman is all about attraction. Yes, you want to be able to catch the attention of the right man at the right moment. But you also want to encourage that man to act on his attraction to you.

Have you ever caught a guy noticing you? You see him checking you out and you're into it. You quickly check for a ring and don't see one on his finger. So, you play it cool and subtly send out your signals indicating interest and availability. And he's giving off signals of interest, too. But somehow nothing happens? You both leave the premises and never see each other again. As you walk away, you wonder if you're missing out on a great love or your soulmate.

Not surprisingly, I've experienced this before. I used to take the 6 train to midtown for work. Subway rides were always a hassle, but the morning commute was the worst. I would sit and read or listen to music as the train jostled from side to side and from stop to stop. Naturally, the routine got tiring quickly. But one day, I looked up and noticed a man, towering over the head of one of the beggars. He was a handsome man with intense eyes, and he looked at me like he wanted to snatch me up right then and there.

Every morning I'd see this man on the platform, then in the train car. He would stare at me hard, glance away, then glance back. Then I would get off at my stop. Finally, I'd enough of playing this cat and mouse game with him. So, I decided to get magic involved. I began to carry this talisman with me. When I happened to see him watching me again, I smiled, and he smiled back. Then he waltzed right over and started a conversation! Once again, I thanked my hard work and enjoyed the benefits. In the end, we went on a few dates but there was nothing there, but that's life, right?

Anyhow, carrying this talisman with you will increase the likelihood of having romantic interaction with those you desire. You could also throw it into the bath before a big date or a night out to make yourself more alluring.

We'll summon the goddess Venus to empower the talisman. Venus is an immensely popular Roman goddess of love. She's had countless works of art (Venus de Milo and Botticelli's Birth of Venus), music ('80s pop song "Venus"), and modern culture (lends her name to a planet and women's razors) dedicated to her. Because of her notoriety, her name has power!

You will need

- Dried rose petals – for drawing love
- High John the conqueror – for love, luck, and success
- Vetiver – to make you attractive to the opposite sex
- Juniper – for love and to increase male potency
- Dried orange peel – for luck and love
- Myrtle – for love and its association with Venus
- Carnelian stone – to bolster courage, increase confidence and stimulate sexual impulses
- Small pink sachet
- Rose incense – for love

Timing

On a Friday, during a waxing moon

Procedure

1. Ground and center.

2. Cast a circle and call the four quarters.

3. In a mortar, grind together the herbs and flowers. As you grind the herbs, think of being the center of attention. Hold the carnelian and imagine being irresistible to men. Imagine that attractive men are compelled to talk to you. Then add all items into the sachet. Light the incense and hold the sachet over the smoke.

4. Call on Venus to empower the bag by saying:

Venus, Roman goddess of love, beauty, and seduction, I call to you. Give your energy to this talisman, so that it attracts the admiration of the opposite sex. Make me alluring, compelling, and magnetic to men who come near me. Venus, lucky Venus, make me lucky in love. I thank you. Go in peace.

Attract the Right Man for Love

Let's just get this out of the way: to attract true love, you need to let go of the past hurts, slights, disappointment, and insecurities. Have you been hurt in love? It doesn't matter. Have you been cheated on and lied to repeatedly? It doesn't matter. Have you struggled to keep a one-sided relationship going? It doesn't matter. Always the bridesmaid and never the bride? It doesn't matter. It's time to move past it.

I have a super close relationship with my aunt. I grew up with her and she's like a second mother to me. She has a son, my cousin, whom I'm also tight with. Unfortunately, his father wasn't the greatest man; in fact, he was a deadbeat with several women and children around town. How my aunt got involved with him I'll never know. I think it may have been something many of us suffer from –ignorance. Many of us don't know that we can do better. She didn't know how a man should treat a woman he loves. This problem seems to have worsened in recent years. Some of us don't even know what a date *is* nowadays, thanks to hookup culture.

Anyhow, over the past 25 years, my lovely aunt has only ever "dated" one other man and that was very briefly. As I got older, I noticed more and more that my loving, caring, hardworking aunt was always alone. Finally, I asked her (delicately) why she didn't date. Apparently, a man she dated had jokingly called her an "old lady" because she was a couple of years older than he was. This one comment was so hurtful that she never forgot it. Since then, she gave up on men completely, and thought of them as "no good."

I couldn't believe that she held onto one small slight all these years. I couldn't fathom that she used it as a reason to give up on love. Ladies, you have to let go and be ready to dust yourself off and try again.

And when you're ready to open up to love again, use this spell!

You will need

* Pink male and female candles – for love

- Olive oil – for potency
- Caraway – to attract a mate
- Dried lemon peel – for longevity and friendship
- Vervain – for love and to attract lovers
- Jasmine – to attract a spiritual love
- Cumin – to ensure fidelity
- Pink rose petals – to draw love
- Basil – for love, protection, and happiness
- Dried orange peel – for love and good luck
- High John the conqueror – to bring success
- Dragon's blood incense – increase potency
- A rose quartz heart – to attract love and open the heart chakra
- Knight of Cups tarot card – represents the special man
- Ace of Cups tarot card – signifies a new relationship
- The Lovers tarot card – for love
- Two of Cups tarot card – for a strong bond and commitment
- Ten of Pentacles – a well-established relationship
- A plate
- Parchment paper – for your petition

Timing

Begin on a Friday during a waxing moon (best to finish on the full moon)

Procedure

1. Ground and center.

2. Cast a circle and call the four quarters.

3. Sit and think of the type of man you desire for a partner. Think of the qualities he'll have. Think about the type of relationship you want to have with him. Write it all down on a piece of paper.

4. In a mortar, combine all the herbs. As you add each herb, hold it briefly in your and reflect on why you are adding it, which property you're conjuring. Grind the mixture together as much as possible. The orange peel will probably still be whole, but that's perfectly fine.

5. Take the female candle and with a pin inscribe your name. You should also add your astrological sign. State the intention that this represents you. Anoint the candle with olive oil and place aside.

6. Then take the male candle in hand. State the intention that it represents your desired partner. Anoint the male candle. Remember to stroke toward yourself to draw the love to you.

7. Pour the mixture onto the plate and roll each candle in the herbs. Set the candles on the plate (make sure this

is done on a stable surface). Turn the candles so that they face each other.

8. Place the tarot cards in front of the candles and set rose quartz heart in front of the pair.

9. Next, write your petition on the parchment paper. Your petition should avoid words like "I want" or "I will." It should be written in the present tense. For example, "I have a loving partner who adores me."

10. Light the dragon's blood incense and light the candles. Read your petition out loud.

11. Visualize yourself with the man of your dreams. See yourself together with him doing all the things you'd do if you were in a relationship. Place yourself there and feel the feeling of having the relationship you desire.

12. Say the following:

Aphrodite, bring new love to me:
A man of my dreams, a man of my desires.
Call him forth speedily.
Call him forth now, I'm ready.
Oh, great Aphrodite, bring my love to me.
As I will it, so shall it be.
I thank you, mighty Aphrodite!

13. Work this spell for 7 days for 15- 20 minutes each night. On the final night, after you have read your petition, fold it three times. Fold it in half toward you, then turn

it slightly clockwise, and fold it again. Repeat again until you've folded it three times.

14. Set the petition alight and place it in a heat-proof container to burn. Once the candles have burned down, bury the remaining candle wax and ashes.

Attracting New Friends

This may seem like a weird spell to include in the love section of the book, but love isn't only about romance and sexual pleasure. Friendships are important because having a large circle of friends can assist you in countless ways, including finding love. When I moved off to college, my friendships helped to sustain me. And when I left the big city for greener pastures, my new friends helped me survive. And in the rat race and struggle to the top, my friends kept me mentally emotionally and spiritually stable.

Unfortunately, I think many Black women tend to keep some friendships far past their expiration dates. It could be because it's hard for us to move out of our comfort zone. Or maybe we feel we don't have the time or energy to devote to making new friends? But lack of time is a sorry excuse.

You need this spell if your group of friends hasn't changed since college. You need this spell if you think you have terrible luck with female friendships. You especially need this spell if you have a business that you're working to get off the ground. Try it for yourself!

You will need

- ❀ Three of Cups tarot card – to represent supportive female friendship
- ❀ Tarot card representing yourself
- ❀ Yellow ribbon
- ❀ A white candle

Timing

On a Friday, Monday or Sunday, New Moon, Moon in Aquarius or Leo

Procedure

1. Perform this ritual outside in a wooded area or park.

2. Ground and center.

3. Cast a circle and call the four quarters.

4. Stand or sit in front of a tree.

5. Place the Three of Cups on the left and your signifier card on the right.

6. Set the ribbon and candle between them.

7. Say the following as you gaze into the flame:

   Green man of the forest, it is new friends I seek.
   Friendships that will support and uplift me
   Vibrant, friends who will enliven dull weeks
   Tight bonds that will sustain me on my journey

As I rise to reach my peak

8. Move the two tarot cards together and place the ribbon on top. Meditate on the type of friendship you desire or on what friendship means to you.

9. Write on the ribbon: Draw uplifting new friends to me.

10. Take the ribbon and tie it to a branch.

11. Say: Thank you. Now go in peace.

Chapter 6

*I'm blessed by the universe,
the source of my abundance.*

"It's the green, it's the green, it's the green you
need and when I looking into
your eyes it's the green that I see"

The Princess and the Frog, Dr. Facilier

The Doc expressed the situation plainly and clearly: 'the green' is often what we think we need to improve our situation. However, focusing on 'the green' can often times be shortsighted. When we think we need 'the green,' what we usually mean is that we need a change in circumstances that will allow 'the green' to flow more abundantly into our lives. But to change circumstances, you need to ask for not only an increase in pay but also an increase in cash flow, opportunities, connections and good luck. You need to remove any blockages that could be hindering your expansion and you must automate continuous financial growth. Let this section assist you on that journey to your end goal of acquiring more of 'the green!

Angel Sachiel to Find a New Job

I could talk about jobs forever. Most people want a job they can be proud of, that's challenging, rewarding, and fulfilling. However, finding that perfect job can be tricky. It may take a lot of trial and error. If you're lucky, you could land your dream job fairly quickly. You may be in the right place at the right time or have the right connections. But for many, the process could take years.

Tamara, a friend of mine, spent seven years bouncing from one dead-end job to the next. She wanted a managerial marketing position. She had a degree in Marketing Management, she was highly intelligent and a fast learner. And she was eager to prove herself. After three years, she had sufficient experience, but her lucky break never came. In fact, she left marketing altogether because she became so disillusioned with the industry.

Thankfully, she was able to find a dream job and the success she desired once she left marketing to become a realtor. However, that realization came after seven years of unnecessary struggle. You could avoid making a similar mistake by using magic to give you an edge!

For this spell, you'll be calling on the Angel Sachiel to help you get a new job. Although I love working with angel energies, I know that many black witches avoid it. For some of us, angel magic reminds us of the Judeo-Christian BS we left behind. It reminds us of our past love of white baby Jesus.

However, it helps to know that the concept of angels predates the Judeo-Christian belief system. Angels or angel-like beings show up in many cultures across the globe.

Sachiel is the archangel of abundance and the harvest. His name means "covering of God." He's the angel of Thursday and therefore rules expansion and all financial matters. His power helps you earn money, thus giving him influence over careers. However, you must make an effort for this angel to work for you.

You will need

- ❀ A light blue candle
- ❀ Sage incense
- ❀ Cedar essential oil (if you have it)
- ❀ A tin box
- ❀ Blue ink pen
- ❀ Parchment paper

Timing

On a Thursday, during a waxing moon

Procedure

1. Ground and center.

2. Cast a circle and call the four quarters.

3. Write out in detail everything you want your job to be and everything you don't want. Avoid using words like "no," "not," or "don't." The Universe doesn't understand negatives. For example, "I don't want drama in my workplace" is a negative way of phrasing this request. Instead, the sentence can be stated positively: "I want a drama-free workplace."

4. Fold the petition three times. Fold it in half toward you, then turn it slightly clockwise, and fold it again. Repeat again until you've folded it three times.

5. Carve the symbol of archangel Sachiel or of Jupiter onto the candle and anoint it with a bit of cedar essential oil. Light the candle and the sage incense.

6. Say the following:

    By the power of Adoni, I call to you Sachiel, lord of Jupiter, angel of expansion, and career. Sachiel, whose name means "covering of God," come be with me now. Hear my plea. I ask that you bring me a new job that fulfills all my needs. Bring me this new and fulfilling job now, Sachiel. By your grace, grant me my request, Sachiel. I thank you.

7. Place the petition in the tin box. Put the candle in a candle holder and let the candle burn down. Ensure the box is cool before touching it.

8. Pour the melted wax on the box to seal it then store it in a cool dry place.

9. Continue your job search knowing that the power of the angel is aiding you in your search. Know that you'll find the type of job you desire.

Quick Cash

Guess what? Your car just broke down and needs to be taken to the shop. No worries, you're a responsible adult, so you always save for a rainy day. You should be fine right? Well, guess what? Your child **and** the cat have the flu. No worries, it may be tight, but you can make it through. But, guess what...

Yes, ladies, no matter how careful and responsible we are, there are times when we can be blindsided by events. Sometimes everything seems to go wrong at once. If you have an emergency and cash is needed, try this little spell below:

You'll be calling on Oshun, a Yoruba goddess. Oshun is the Orisha of love, money, sweet waters and wealth.

You will need

- ❀ An orange
- ❀ Honey
- ❀ Yellow candle

Procedure

1. Ground and center.

2. Cast a circle and call the four quarters.

3. At your altar, say the following:

   Oshun, hear my plea:
   I need money fast, let it come to me.
   Minute by minute, hour by hour;
   Let money flow to me.
   Money, let me see,
   As I will it, so let it be!

4. Cut the orange into 4 quarters and drizzle it with honey.

5. Place the offering on your altar and say:

   I offer this in thanks. Thank you.

Favorite Cord Spell

I know what you're thinking- cord spells are boring. There are so many cord spells out there, so why include one in this book? Because, although cord spells may be simple, common, and a little boring, they **are** effective. How do cord spells work and why do they work? Cord spells work because you're focusing your intention into the cord and binding that intention with the knot you create.

Cord spells can be as simple or as intricate as you'd like. Some cord spells require you to tie many knots and undo one each week until you reach your goal. Others incorporate numerology to help you achieve your goal. There are cord spells that compel you to call various deities for assistance. And some of the more intricate cord spells use multiple cords to form a weaving pattern.

When I first learned about cord spells, I was skeptical.

Now I love them and have used them to bring various things to me numerous times. Try this one for yourself:

You will need

- ⚜ A long green or gold cord
- ⚜ A candle
- ⚜ Any incense (money incense)

Procedure

1. Ground and center.

2. Cast a circle and call the four quarters.

3. As you tie a knot state the following;

By knot of one, my money spell is spun.
By knot of two, the Universe will make it true.
By knot of three, money comes to me.

By knot of four, open the door.
By knot of five, the spell's alive.
By knot of six, this is just the fix.
By knot of seven, money fall from Heaven.
By knot of eight, open the floodgates.
By knot of nine, the spell's done: now's the time.

It is done. Carry the cord with you until you receive the money.

Ganesha to Remove Obstacles to Wealth

Before I talk about removing obstacles, I should define what I mean when I use the word "wealth."

According to Merriam-Webster, wealth is an "abundance of valuable material possessions or resources" ("Wealth," Merriam-Webster, 2019).

This makes sense. When you think of wealth, you usually envision having a lot of stuff. For example, you may think about having a fancy car, big house, boats, designer clothing, and a nice chunk of change in your bank account.

However, there's another definition provided by Merriam-Webster. There's the financial or business definition of wealth. It is, "Wealth is usually a measure of net worth... it is a measure of how much a person has in savings, investments, real estate, and cash, less any debts." Furthermore, it states "Income is routinely mistaken for wealth" ("Wealth," Merriam-Webster, 2019).

I think many Black women have an abundance of the first type of wealth. But many of us are lacking in the second type. Unfortunately, because of the way the world works, many obstacles could prevent Black women from acquiring the second type of wealth. It may be one of the trifectas: sexism, classism, or racism. Or obstacles to wealth could include lack of access, lack of connections, lack of resources, or even unfortunate geographic location.

Or it could be the two biggest obstacles to success? What are the two biggest obstacles to success? They are fear and ignorance. That's right, not knowing what you don't know could block you from acquiring wealth. And being afraid of taking risks could prevent you from acquiring wealth.

My friend April missed out on a possibly life-changing investment because she didn't understand how the stock market worked. She was still traumatized from the 2008 financial collapse and, acting out of fear, decided to hold on to her money. So, she let the investment opportunity pass her.

A family member was a damn good baker and dreamed of opening and running her own bakery. In the end, she deemed it too impractical because of the startup costs. Instead, she settled for a 9-5 job she hates. She was ignorant about grants provided to minority business. She feared failure, and it cost her.

Use Ganesha to overcome these obstacles and allow the second type of wealth to flow into your life. Now, this ritual won't give you a payload of cash, but it'll work to clear away some of the factors blocking you from acquiring wealth. Ganesha is the famous elephant-headed Hindu god. He's the god of arts and sciences, intellect, and wisdom. He's also known as the remover of obstacles.

You will need

- A framed photo of Ganesha
- Yellow flowers
- A red candle
- Ganesha incense, if you have any

Procedure

1. Ground and center.

2. Cast a circle and call the four quarters.

3. Place the photo in the center and the place the candle in front of the image.

4. Light the candle. Gaze at the candle as you chant AUM. After a few minutes state the following:

   Ganesha, the elephant-headed god of arts and sciences, of intellect and wisdom. Ganesha, you who are revered as the remover of obstacles. Ganesha, lord of hosts, I call to you now in my time of need to remove all obstacles blocking wealth from flowing to me. Lift all obstacles, oh Ganesha, clear them now so that prosperity and wealth will come to me.

5. Lay the flowers on the altar.

   I leave these flowers as an offering; please accept them as thanks for your assistance. Ganesha, remover of obstacles, Lord of hosts, I thank you. Go in peace.

114

Money Charm Bag

Yes, we want the great job and it's useful to be able to attract cash quickly. However, consistent cash flow is the key.

The financial collapse happened to coincide with my college graduation. I remember it like it was yesterday. I was handed my diploma and looked forward to starting my climb to the top and an illustrious career. I'd accepted an offer from a midsized company and was eager to begin at the end of the month. I was also looking forward to the small break. But in the blink of an eye, circumstances changed. My offer evaporated and the economy imploded. Day after day, another prominent, supposedly rock-solid financial institution went under. It seemed like Armageddon. Although things did bounce back, I never forgot the feeling of sheer panic as people lost their jobs.

This is illustrative of why it's important to have multiple income streams. The steady flow of cash will be a great comfort to you. You'll know that you won't be in a position where a loss of employment will make you destitute.

If you want money to constantly and continually flow into your life, you must attract it there. You can create this little charm bag and place it in your wallet. Carry it everywhere with you and you'll notice that money and opportunities to make money will flow to you. Please note that you'll need to recharge the charm every so often.

You will need

- Two 3-inch squares of green felt

- A square piece of paper
- Green thread
- Needle
- High John – to attract money
- 6 crushed cashews – for money
- Cedar – to draw wealth
- Fenugreek – to bring money into the household
- Ginger – to ensure the success of a magical operation
- Dried orange peel – good luck
- Cedar essential oil – to draw money
- Tiger's eye – to promote wealth and money

Procedure

1. Ground and center.

2. Cast a circle and call the four quarters.

3. Sew the two pieces of felt together, leaving the top open.

4. On the paper write an affirmation or a little incantation or draw a sigil. Fold the paper three times. Fold it in half toward you, then turn it slightly clockwise and fold it again. Repeat again until you've folded it three times.

5. Slip the other items into the pouch.

6. Sew the top closed. Sew until the square is sealed, keeping your intention firmly in mind. Think of money coming to you from unknown and unexpected sources.

7. Once you're done, light your incense. Anoint the bag with a bit of cedar oil.

8. Hold the bag over the incense to catch the rising smoke. As you do this, recite Psalm 119, 17-24:

"Deal bountifully with thy servant, that I may live, and keep thy word.

Open thou mine eyes, that I may behold wondrous things out of thy law.

I am a stranger in the earth: hide not thy commandments from me.

My soul breaketh for the longing that it hath unto thy judgments at all times.

Thou hast rebuked the proud that are cursed, which do err from thy commandments.

Remove from me reproach and contempt; for I have kept thy testimonies.

Princes also did sit and speak against me: but thy servant did meditate in thy statutes.

Thy testimonies also are my delight and my counselors."

Remember to keep your mind focused on prosperity coming to you. Once the bag is made, keep it in your purse or wallet and carry it with you always.

Good Luck with Money

What do I mean when I talk about having luck with money? It's more than just finding a five-dollar bill on the street. I mean overall good fortune. Money luck influences all financial matters. Have you ever gone to the store to buy milk and noticed that the milk was half-off the day before? Or maybe you longed for a YSL handbag, ran out, and purchased it at full price right before the seasonal clearance? These seem like small things, but they add up over time. And it has to do with having good fortune.

Lakshmi is the most popular Hindu goddess in India. She's the goddess of wealth, fortune, and prosperity. Images often portray her as a woman with golden skin, wearing red and gold embroidered garments. She has four arms that are usually covered in bangles and golden coins flow from her hands. To her followers, she symbolizes good luck. By calling on Lakshmi, you invite her into your life to change your fortune.

You will need

- 6 pennies – Lakshmi is often depicted with golden coins
- Frame
- Picture of Lakshmi

- One green candle – a color associated with Lakshmi
- One pink candle – a color associated with Lakshmi
- Unlined paper
- Green pen – to symbolize wealth, money and riches
- Any pleasant incense

Procedure

1. Ground and center.

2. Cast a circle and call the four quarters.

3. Place the picture of Lakshmi in the frame and set on your altar.

4. Light the two candles and incense.

5. On the paper, write Lakshmi's mantra:

   Om Shrim Maha Lakshmiyei Namaha.

6. Write the following below the mantra:

   Lakshmi, give me good luck in all money matters.

7. Chant the following mantra 108 times:

   Om Shreem Mah-hah Lahk-shmee-yea Nama-hah

8. As you chant, imagine Lakshmi and see golden coins cascading from her hands.

9. When you are finished thank Lakshmi and pinch out the candles. Perform the ritual for 6 days.

10. Afterward, fold the coins in the petition, and bury it.

Money Drawing Powder

I was a child the first time I heard about magic powders. I overheard some adults talking about "throwing powder." It was a warning to beware of someone throwing powder in your path. I had no idea that they were referring to witchcraft and magic. The idea of powder didn't seem dangerous enough to warrant a warning, so. I dismissed it as foolish superstition.

However, years later, after I began practicing magic, this memory came back to me. I thought it must be powerful magic if my Christian family knew to avoid it. Since then, I've incorporated magic powders into my practice in my ways. Here's a simple formula for you to try for yourself:

You will need

- ❈ High John the conqueror – to attract money
- ❈ Ginger (fresh or powder) – to add power to a spell and to attract money
- ❈ Black tea leaves – to ensure future riches
- ❈ Sweet flag – to protect against poverty
- ❈ Tiger's eye – to charge the powder with money attracting energy
- ❈ Dragon's blood incense – to increase spell's potency
- ❈ Small bottle with cover – to store the powder

Procedure

1. Ground and center.

2. Cast a circle and call the four quarters.

3. In a mortar, combine the high john, jasmine, sweet flag, and ginger together. It's okay to transfer to an electrical grinder to make the materials into a powder.

4. Burn the black tea leaves in a fire-proof bowl and add the ashes to the mix.

5. Light your incense. Hold the bottle over the incense to let in the smoke.

6. Empower the tiger's eye by holding it tightly in your hand and pouring your psychic energy into the stone.

7. Place the stone into the bottle and pour in the powdered mixture.

8. Sit at your altar and chant the following three times as you shake the bottle:

Money and wealth, now come to me,
By Earth and Air, by Fire and Sea.
This powder works to draw riches to me.
As I will it, so shall it be!

You can draw money to you by sprinkling this powdered mix of herbs in key locations. Sprinkle some of this powder in your shoes, in your wallet or near the entrance of your home. You can also use this to dress candles and put it in mojo bags.

Prosperity Oil

Here's a little secret, prosperity isn't just about cold hard cash. No, it's about an abundance of all good things linked to economic success. The key here is success and success is largely a mindset- a vibrational frequency that can be tapped into in order to draw more success. Now, as witches, we should know the importance of attuning and aligning our vibrational frequency to our desires so that we can manifest those desires into our reality. Well, this is exactly what this oil does.

One of the biggest blocks that kept me in 'the struggle' was the feeling of poverty and struggle that hung over my every thought. It affected my attitude towards everything in my life and worked to warp my perception. Of course, as I vibrated, powerfully, the feeling of struggle, hardship and lack all these circumstances became my constant reality. I knew I needed to turn this around, so I took a step back and asked the universe to show me how to change my vibrational frequency to allow for prosperity. I was led to quite a few methods that helped me flip that unwanted energy on its head. In sum, this is oil was one of the quickest and easy methods I developed.

The greatest perk about the oil is that it increases the sense of having more than enough, of having and being able to have, all your needs and desires met right now. Getting your needs met will no longer feel like a struggle for you because you'll feel as though you are already prospering. Just wearing the oil will change your vibrational frequency to one of prosperity, which will draw new opportunities in all aspects of life.

You will need

- ❀ Peppermint essential oil – for prosperity
- ❀ Olive oil – to increase potency
- ❀ Cinnamon – for success and to draw money
- ❀ Cloves – to attract riches
- ❀ Small quartz crystal – to charge with intent (tiger's eye or citrine may be substituted)
- ❀ Green glitter or gold – colors of wealth and riches
- ❀ Menstrual blood – to increase potency and tie spell to your energy
- ❀ Small glass jar
- ❀ Small glass essential oil bottle in a dark color
- ❀ Cheesecloth – to strain oil
- ❀ Small funnel

Timing

Waxing moon, Tuesday, Thursday or Sunday

Procedure:

1. On a night of the waxing moon, gather together ingredients.

2. Ground and center.

3. Cast a circle and call the four quarters.

4. Using the glitter, draw the Earth symbol on both the glass jar and essential oil bottle.

5. Next, hold the crystal in your hand and charge it with your intent before adding it into the jar.

6. Do the same for the cinnamon and cloves before adding them to the jar.

7. Pour 4 ounces of olive into the jar over the items completely covering them.

8. Next, add 4 drops of peppermint essential oil to the mixture.

9. Cover the mixture and leave it in a cool dark place for at least a month.

10. On the night of the next full moon during the hour of Jupiter, sit at your altar, ground, center, and call the four quarters.

11. Strain the mixture into a container and then funnel the final mixture into the essential oil bottle

12. Next, add a few drops of your menstrual blood.

13. Add the glitter into the bottle swirling it in a clockwise motion. As you do so, imagine money and riches swirling into your life and all around you.

14. Bless the mixture with the following as you lift the bottle to each corner:

   I bless you by the power of Earth.
   I bless you by the power of Air.
   I bless you by the power of Fire.
   I bless you by the power of Water.

15. Place the bottle back on your altar and invoke Jupiter to empower it with the following

   I call on the energy of Jupiter, of expansion and prosperity to infuse this oil with its energy. Empower this mixture so that it draws prosperity, money, and expansion of all good things in life.

Label and store the oil in a cool dark place. You can wear this oil daily, on Thursday's, while performing money rituals or use it to anoint candles.

General Good Luck Ritual

I have a male friend named Anthony. Well, Anthony was born lucky. He was born a white male to a middle-class family in the USA (a boon, let's not pretend it isn't). He had the perfect home life and drama free upbringing (a dream life really). But that isn't what truly makes him lucky. You see, whenever Anthony needs or desires anything, it simply comes to him. And it's almost always the best! Whenever he dislikes something, it simply disappears from his life. It happens quickly - without fuss.

For example, after years of being indifferent to sports in high school, he figured he needed an extracurricular to appeal to colleges. However, he didn't want to choose a contact sport. And he was still was mulling it over when a member of the track team suffered an injury. He tried out and was immediately accepted for the team. Coincidently becoming a track star earned him a nice scholarship. Books paid for and everything!

When he was lost in that first year of college (like so many are) and he didn't know which career path to choose he happened to wander into a Church service that held quite a few prominent members of a particular Christian denomination. A few of these special members owned a multi-million-dollar family business and happened to like him. He was down for a place to belong. Before long, he was all up in the mix, attending socials, being invited to members' home, and of course being gifted with the opportunity to intern then work at the family business.

His was set on a lucrative career path, **FROM HIS FRESHMAN YEAR** all because he just happened into a church service. To cap it off, he ended up meeting and marrying his wife as a result.

After listening to Anthony's stories again and again, I began to hate the guy (And still love him because he's a sweetheart), but I couldn't help but think of how different my story is from his own. I'd meditate on the different ways that lady luck had dropped the ball in my life but seemed to be best friends with Anthony. Besides, he wasn't the only one. I've met people of all colors, sexes, and backgrounds who just seem to have been born lucky. Fate just always lined up for them in a way that led to their greatest benefit.

One day, after hearing Anthony complain about his job and how management didn't want to grow the company, so he was forced to do nothing all day and receive a large salary. I was trying to repress the urge to roll my eyes when it hit me: The Universe sent Anthony to me at that time in my life me for a reason. It was after I became a practicing witch and had a few years under my belt but still struggled with the idea of struggling. I was moving from thinking that 'the struggle' was just the way life was to thinking that I had been duped and wondering how to get out that paradigm.

Anthony's life was meant to open my eyes to how good life could be. He was meant to serve as an example for how things could align for me if got serious about directing the flow of energy in my life. After confronting the intense well of resentment I had for these lucky people, I thanked the Universe for showing me its immense possibilities. Then I developed a simple ritual that could be performed routinely to allow good luck to flow into my life:

You will need

- One green candle
- Quartz crystal chips – for charging candle and spell
- Ground nutmeg – to bring good luck
- Sweet flag – to draw good luck
- Echinacea – to strengthen spell
- Prosperity oil – see formula

- ❀ Paper for petition
- ❀ Dragon's blood incense – for potency

Timing

During the new or waxing moon or Sunday

Procedure

1. Ground and center.

2. Cast a circle and call the four quarters.

3. On inch wide strip of petition paper, write your desire for you luck to change.

4. On the candle, carve the words, "good luck for me," on the candle several times.

5. Grind the roots together into a powder using a mortar and pestle.

6. Dress the candle using olive oil and ground mixture. As you do so, keep your intent firmly in mind.

7. Next, wrap the petition paper around the bottom of the candle (the oil will help it stick).

8. Encircle the candle with the quartz crystal chips.

9. Finally, light your candle and gaze into the flame. Now it's time to visualize. Don't just visualize getting something you desire. You need to feel the accompanying emotion you get when an unexpected gift shows up in

your life. The feeling is one of joy mixed with pleasant surprise. It's the feeling that makes you say out loud, "what luck" or "f@#k yeah." Hold on to that feeling as you visualize your life turning into a storm of happy coincidences. Retain that feeling as you gaze into the candle flame.

10. Now chant the words of your petition as follows:

   By Earth, Air, Fire and Water [state petition].
   As I will it, so let it be!

11. After 15-20 minutes pinch out the flame. Repeat this for three days.

12. On the third day, allow the candle to burn down and bury the remnants at a crossroads.

Chapter 7

Healing Spells

My mind, body, and spirit are in harmonic alignment with the goodness of the universe.

In Chapter 1 we discussed the need for us to be focused on our wellbeing as Black witches. Well, we're only human and as humans we're far from perfect. Sometimes despite our best intentions, illness, ailment, disease or maladies can happen. Other times what ails us in not easily treatable as the cause is rooted deep in past traumas or mental and spiritual anguish. Whatever may happen or has occurred, it's your duty to seek help and healing for yourself. And, if you're wise, you'll do so as quickly as a possible.

An important note on healing spells and rituals: They aren't a substitute for medical treatment. Please don't forgo seeking immediate medical help if you have any medical issue. Magic is an aid and should be used as an addition to proper medical care and treatment.

Prayer to Raphael for General Healing

Raphael is one of my favorite angels. His energy is truly miraculous. He's the archangel of travel and healing. Raphael's name means "God has healed." He rules Wednesday, and the color associated with him is yellow. He's also associated with lavender, lemon balm and lemongrass fragrances.

For years, I suffered from this constant ache in the center of my forehead. This wasn't good, as it is where the third eye chakra is located. I suffered in silence and eventually the pain/discomfort became a normal part of my life.

I just happened to complain about the pain to my doctor, and he suggested an MRI. I took his advice and had the procedure. As a result, I found out that I had a slightly deviated septum. This caused the constant pain/discomfort I'd experienced most of my life.

The doctor presented two possible solutions. I could ignore it because it wasn't life-threatening, or I could opt for a nose job to fix the deviated septum! Both of these were out of the question, so I turned to Raphael for assistance. I felt his presence as soon as I began the ritual.

In this simple ritual, you'll call on him to aid in healing:

You will need

⊛ A yellow candle

- ❀ Lavender, lemon balm or lemongrass essential oil
- ❀ Primrose incense

Procedure

1. Ground and center.

2. Cast a circle and call the four quarters.

3. Light the incense. Anoint the yellow candle with the essential oil, while keeping your intent in mind.

4. Sit quietly and think of the issue that needs healing. Once you have that feeling, light your candle and say the following:

   Raphael archangel of healing, I request your aid. Raphael, archangel of Wednesday, I ask you to be here with me. Raphael, whose name means God has healed, hear me.

   Raphael, my need is great, so I call to you in this hour. Help to heal what ails me and bless me with your healing touch.

5. Now imagine a glowing yellow light enter your body from the crown of your head. Think of it as Raphael's healing light. Visualize this light traveling throughout your body until your entire body glows. See the light pulsating within you and imagine it dissolving all ailments in your body.

6. Now imagine that you're completely healed. See yourself living life happy, healthy and whole. Feel the joy, relief, and gratitude of being healed. Sit with this feeling as you watch the flame. When you're ready, say aloud the following:

Raphael, great healer, I thank you for your aid. Go in peace.

7. Work this ritual for 3 days. Then let the candle burn down completely.

To Help Heal Childhood Wounds

We all have childhood wounds. Everyone on the planet has experienced something in their youth that has stayed with them well into adulthood. I'd like to share one of mine. It's a common one among Black girls. It has to do with my hair, so it's not shocking at all.

Every Sunday my mother and I would endure the ritual of doing my hair for the week. My mother was not fussy about appearance, so she didn't particularly enjoy doing my hair. That meant that she wasn't particularly careful when handling my hair.

Sunday night became fight night in my house as she struggled with me and I struggled with her. One day she had enough and told me I was going to get my hair done at the salon. She dropped me off and picked me up eight hours later (Black salon problems). She told the stylist to give me braids and I thought nothing of it. I was just happy that Sunday fight night had come to an end.

The next day, I went to school feeling pretty happy with my new hairstyle. Unfortunately, the class clown/bully thought my new hairstyle was hideous and took every opportunity to tease me about it. By the end of the day, he encouraged the entire class to start calling me "Whoopi." With that one word, I became insecure about not only my hair but also my features and skin color. I took the braids out after a week, but the lingering feelings of shame, low self-worth, and helplessness remained with me for a very long time.

I thought I was over it until a friend offhandedly remarked that I was beautiful. Suddenly, I started to cry. The floodgates had opened, and all of that pent-up emotion came out. I realized I had to do something about it. So, I developed the ritual below to help me begin to heal my childhood wounds.

You will need

- A fat light purple candle – purple for healing
- 4 quartz crystal points – to amplify the healing energy
- A symbol of your childhood
- Paper
- Pen

Procedure

1. Ground and center.

2. Cast a circle and call the four quarters.

3. On the paper, write truthfully about the issue. Really pour out your soul. Describe the incident or event in great detail. Recall specifically how it made you feel, then about how it changed you. Write about how the past trauma affects you today.

4. Surround the purple candle with the crystal points. Light your candle.

5. Read your letter out loud and then say the following:

    May the pain of the past leave me on this day;
    I release the guilt, anger, sorrow, and pain.
    From now on, only peace will remain.
    Let air blow the pain away!
    Let fire scorch the hurt away!
    Let water wash the pain away!
    Let the Earth bury my grief today!
    Pain and trauma, now burn away;
    So, peace and happiness can now stay!

6. Gaze into the flame of the candle. Cup your hands over the flame, close enough to feel the warmth but not close enough to burn. See a warm healing purple light emanating from the candle. Imagine the purple light moving into you, flowing from your hands, up your arms, into your chest and engulfing your heart.

7. Work this ritual for 3 days. On the third day, light the paper on fire using the candle. Let it burn in a fire-proof cauldron or fire-proof container. As it burns, feel

the emotional pain lift and see it burning away gradually.

8. Let the candle burn down completely. Bury the wax and ashes.

Reveal Your True Self

Do you know yourself? Many people don't know who they really are. I'm talking about the real you, not the mask of overachiever, mother, daughter, professional, or teacher. The real you, under all the goals, achievements, lies, self-deceptions, and self-delusions. Many of us delude ourselves. We like to think we're better than we truly are. We're hiding inside a hollow outer shell.

We know that we should love ourselves; it's in every self-help book out there. But when you repeat the affirmation in the latest self-help book, designed to get you to love yourself, what "self" do you mean? Can you describe your "self" satisfactorily to others? If I asked you to introduce yourself today, what would you say? Would you know what to say? Would your description include how many degrees you have under your belt? Would your description include wife and mother? Student or friend? Is it enough to know your role in relation to others?

My dear friend, Jennifer, can rattle off all the degrees she has, the positions she's held, the companies she worked for during her career. She can tell you her political affiliation and who she thinks should be in office. However, she once confided in me that she's unsure if she's fulfilling her life purpose. She's uncertain whether the life she's living is one that she wants for herself or what she thinks she should want.

Now, this is a sad situation, but I don't think it's that uncommon. How many times have you seen someone who is dissatisfied with their life? They forgot to stop and ask, "Is this what I want?" This person may be a high-powered attorney or a janitor. But somewhere along the way, they lost touch with themself. I told Jennifer that the answers lie within her. She has to look within, take an honest view of herself and confront her issues.

It's time to dig deeper. Focus on getting to know you. Try the ritual below to help. It's fairly simple but helpful.

You will need

- ❀ Frankincense incense – aids in spiritual work
- ❀ Quartz crystal – for healing and spiritual work
- ❀ A white candle
- ❀ Pen
- ❀ Paper

Procedure

1. Find a quiet place where you can be alone. Make sure that you're away from any distractions and won't be disturbed.

2. Light the incense. Light the candle.

3. Keep a pen and paper in front of you.

4. Take a gulping deep breath in through your mouth. Breathe out through your nose. Do this twice more.

5. Now, hold the crystal in your hand and chant three times:

   With your beauty and clarity,
   Help me to see what I don't wish to see!

6. Now ask yourself out loud, *"What am I not facing about myself?"* or *"What am I afraid to face about myself?"*

7. This will bring up the usual mundane answers you give others, but don't buy into them. They're merely at the surface, and you wish to go deeper. So, sit in quietness as you hold the crystal.

8. Eventually, the truth will come up. It's usually something you don't want to see about yourself.

9. Write it down. Do this without feeling the need to judge or label.

10. Now you're going to investigate. You're going to question this response like you're a detective.

11. Write down each question and your answer.

12. You should spend at least 15 minutes performing this inner investigation. After you're finished, think of the parts of yourself you've revealed. You may perform the ritual as often as you wish to do so. Each time you will gain new insight into yourself.

Below is an example:

> **Question:** What am I not facing about myself?
> **Answer:** I'm not good enough
>
> **Question:** Why don't I feel good enough?
> **Answer:** Because others are doing better than I am
>
> **Question:** Is that a problem?
> **Answer:** Yes, because it makes me look bad
>
> **Question:** Look bad to whom?
> **Answer:** To friends, colleagues, strangers
>
> **Question:** Is it important what they think?
> **Answer:** Yes, I don't want to look bad because people won't accept me
>
> **Question:** Is it important for people to accept me?
> **Answer:** Yes, of course it is
>
> **Question:** Why?
> **Answer:** Because they can hurt me
>
> **Question:** How?
> **Answer:** By leaving me alone

You can tell from this example that this person has a need to please others, to maintain a certain image, and fears abandonment. These are serious self-worth issues that need to be addressed and dismantled instead of buried within. In fact, the truth will eventually appear, and the emotional fall-out could cause an implosion (depression, anxiety or self-sabotage) in your life.

Tea to Ease Menstrual Pain

If we're going to work on healing pain, then we must address the elephant in the room. Period pain! I know it hurts. I also understand that some Black women suffer from a host of menstrual problems. It may be related to past trauma, but that's a theory for another day.

Over the years, I have witnessed friends, enemies, family members, and colleagues suffer. I've also suffered from this problem. I used to have major cramping for days. It felt like being punched in the stomach repeatedly. Some people may advise us to take painkillers. However, some women may not react well to painkillers. And others, like me, don't like putting chemical substances in our bodies. This tea may be what you need to help you during that time of the month.

You will need

- Peppermint tea leaves – for healing
- Chamomile – to combat curses
- Dried blackberries – for healing
- Honey

Procedure

1. Brew the tea as usual by adding the loose ingredients to hot water. Let seep for 5-7 minutes.

2. Pour tea into a cup.

3. As you add the honey, say the following:

Ease my hurt, banish my pain.
Sweet tea of mine, remove this bane.
By Earth, Air, Fire, and Sea,
As I will it, so shall it be!

Healing Pumpkin Soup

When I was younger, someone in my family tried making pumpkin soup for some reason, but I hated it. So, I stayed away from pumpkin soup for years. However, while visiting a friend's home, I had the opportunity to try it again. I was surprised by how much I enjoyed it. It was delicious and filling, almost magical. So, of course, I begged for the recipe. Unfortunately, it was lost in one of my moves and I kicked myself for not putting somewhere safe. Luckily, I was able to come up with a delicious recipe of my own that's just as good. Try out this magical recipe for yourself.

You will need

- About a pound of fresh pumpkin, chopped
- Olive oil – for healing
- Tablespoon of chopped parsley – for purification
- Tablespoon of chopped basil – for happiness
- Half a head of garlic, chopped – for healing
- One onion diced – for healing
- Salt to taste – cleansing
- Teaspoon of black pepper – protection
- 1 pound of porcini mushrooms

- Half a cup of wild rice
- 2 cups of water
- 4 cups of chicken or vegetable broth

Procedure

1. Heat a large soup pot over medium heat.

2. Pour the olive oil, in a clockwise circle around the pot.

3. Add the mushrooms. Sauté the mushrooms, stirring clockwise, until they're brown. Remove them. Put them on a paper towel on a plate.

4. Add the onions to the pot stirring until golden.

5. Put in the garlic.

6. To the pot, add the pumpkin. Try to make sure that each piece is touching the pan. Cook until you see the edges turn transparent and start to brown.

7. Next, pour in the broth. Stir, making sure that the pumpkin is completely covered by the broth. Cover and let simmer for 5 minutes.

8. After 5 minutes, remove the cover and turn off the stove. With a hand blender, blend the chunks of pumpkin until smooth.

9. Turn the stove back on and add the wild rice, water, and the mushrooms.

10. Let this simmer on the stove for 15-20 minutes or until the rice is soft. Sir it frequently. Remember to keep an eye on the pot, as the soup will start to bubble.

Overcome Humiliation and Shame

We all have moments of embarrassment where we've dropped something or said something foolish. But humiliation and shame are different beasts altogether. Whereas embarrassment is personal and private, humiliation, by its very definition is public and directly linked to the loss of status in your eyes or in the eyes of others.

If you've ever experienced humiliation, then you know that feeling isn't pleasant. Humiliation makes you want to do anything to escape. It can make you feel physically ill and leave lasting scars.

Think of a time you were humiliated. Notice how the feeling is still fresh in your mind, how you react as if you've been punched in the gut. There may be a sinking feeling in your solar plexus or an ache radiating from your neck up to your face. You can still feel it physically because humiliation is traumatic. For example, I know countless Black women who feel like they have to dress a certain way, look a certain way, or speak a certain way. And if you dig beneath the surface, there's usually some link to a past humiliation.

An example is Tia; when she went off to grad school, she inadvertently embarrassed herself by answering a question incorrectly. The embarrassment turned into humiliation when both the teacher and students had a good chuckle at her expense. It seems like a minor issue, but Tia told me that she almost never attempted to answer another question for the remainder of her studies. When she thinks of it, she feels an overwhelming sense of shame. That experience still haunts her because she thinks of how she'll sound to others before she says anything, often missing chances to speak her mind and her truth.

So, don't listen to those who tell you to get over it, that it's in the past, or that it builds character. Because it usually doesn't. Instead, it typically just damages you. And it is important that you deal with past humiliations, so that you can move beyond the trauma to live without the feelings of shame humiliation causes.

You will need

- ❀ The Three of Swords tarot card (use one you can burn) – to represent suffering, regret, and heartache

- ❀ Black candle – to banish

- ❀ Nettle – for exorcism/ keep your demons at bay

- ❀ Rosemary – for exorcism

- ❀ Castor oil – to absorb negativity

Procedure

1. Ground and center.

2. Cast a circle and call the four quarters.

3. Anoint the black candle and dress it with *some* of the herbs.

4. Look at the tarot card. Absorb all of the imagery and, as you do so, think of all the past humiliations haunting you. Imagine them vividly until you can feel them as a physical pain in your body. Pour it into the card.

5. Once you feel the shame and pain leaving your body, take the remaining herbs and sprinkle them onto the card as you state the following:

   Suffering and heartache, I send you away.
   Along with my demons, you shall not stay,
   Humiliation that was brought on me,
   Goes with you, too, so let it be!

6. Continue to chant the incantation as you begin to burn the card slowly. Place it into a fire-proof bowl as it turns to ash.

7. Sprinkle the ashes around the black candle and allow the candle to burn down.

8. Collect the wax and ashes and bury them together

Chapter 8

Protection Spells

*I've turned my life around and
my good decisions direct the flow.*

Ladies, we need to protect ourselves. Being witches means having to take extra precautions as we're more susceptible to the BS surrounding us. And Black women know that we're often surrounded by a storm of BS. It seems to be drawn to us, so we always need to suit up in that armor of protection. Because, when the shit hits the fan, you'll be glad for your magical armor.

Once you've gone through the process of increasing your psychic awareness and tuning yourself into the wonders of the Universe, the last thing you need is to be sideswiped by some event sent in motion by other peoples' messes.

You can also do without the negative energies of unstable persons or leach like attentions of energy vampires out to devour every drop of your carefully cultivated positivity. The rituals and spells below can be used as your first round of defense against the terrors out to disrupt and destroy.

Energy of the Archangels for Protection

If you don't know by now, I should tell you: Angels kick ass! Many people tend to see angels as gentle winged creatures who are there to guide them peacefully down their life paths. But anyone who has actually paid attention to the Bible or other angel literature knows them to be fierce creatures. Yes, they do have peaceful sides, but they're also capable of raining down the wrath of God! You should want them on your side because they're fierce protectors. I call on angels for protection often and they have rescued me from some tough situations.

For example, here's a story that happened to me. Not too long ago, I went back to New York to visit some family and had a great time. We laughed, we ate, we drank, and had a generally enjoyable time. I felt great and wondered why I'd ever let New York. Anyhow, since I was in my hometown again, I decided to get a copy of my birth certificate.

I thought I'd just pop into the New York City Department of Health and Mental Hygiene, pick up the certificate and exit quickly. I trekked downtown to the Department of Health one day during my visit. I'd had a few drinks the night before with my family and paid for it in the morning, so I didn't make it to the downtown office until the afternoon. And I quickly realized why I chose to leave the city. Rude people, loiterers, yelling and cussing greeted me downtown. And the worst part was the woman at the counter.

Now you all know this type of woman: the one with a bitchy attitude for no discernible reason who is determined to make things as difficult as possible for you. She took my info, said there was a problem that needed to be checked, and then proceeded to make me wait for ages. I saw her talking to her supervisor. I'm not sure what was said between them, but she came back with a bigger attitude, asked me a few questions, and told me to wait again.

By this time, I was angry. I'd spent two hours in that department and still didn't have what I'd come for. When she came back, she didn't explain anything, just asked for a fee, handed me everything, and sent me on my way. I was so frustrated and irate by her nonsense that I decided to grab a bite to eat to sooth myself. So, I headed to the train station to make my way down to Chambers Street. As I entered the station, I suddenly had a strong feeling, a hunch, telling me to go back to my family's place. The sensation was so strong that it stopped me in my tracks. I debated what to do for a little while, and then decided that heading back to my family was the better option. So, I got on the opposite train, returned to the house, and ate another hearty meal made by my mother.

So, what the hell was the point of that story? Well, later that night on the news, I saw that there had been a terrorist attack. An unidentified man drove a rented van along the West Street bike path. The attack began at Houston Street and ended at Chambers Street, where he proceeded to exit the van and open fire. Was it all a coincidence? I don't think, so but you can decide for yourself. What I do know is that I was given a warning that stopped me in my tracks. And, because of that, I was able to avoid a seriously dangerous situation. I'm glad I call on angelic protection. Similarly, you can call on them, too.

You will need

- A white candle
- Fragrant flowers of any kind
- Rose, jasmine or lavender incense

Procedure

1. Ground and center.

2. Cast a circle and call the four quarters.

3. Light the candle and incense. State the following:

   Raphael, archangel of healing,
   Raphael, you whose name means 'God has healed,'
   Raphael, archangel of the dawn,
   Raphael who stands in the East,
   I call to you. Be here with me now!

   Uriel, archangel of transformation,
   Uriel, you whose name means 'Fire of God,'
   Uriel, angel of the night,
   Uriel, who stands in the North,
   I call to you. Be here with me now!

Michael, archangel of the light,
Michael, you whose name means 'Who is as God,'
Michael, angel of noonday,
Michael, who stands in the South,
I call to you. Be here with me now!

Gabriel, archangel of the moon,
Gabriel, you whose name means 'God is my Strength,'
Gabriel, angel of evening,
Gabriel, who stands in the West
I call to you. Be here with me now!

Raphael, Uriel, Michael, and Gabriel,
Protect me, be a shield for me against danger,
Shine your light on me and keep me safe from harm!

4. Stare at the candle flame and imagine a white light, glowing and blindingly bright surrounding your entire body.

5. See the white light slowly seeping into your body. Once the light is totally absorbed by your body, visualize yourself glowing from within with this protective energy.

6. Say the following:

Raphael, I thank you!
Uriel, I thank you!
Michael, I thank you!
Gabriel, I thank you!
I bid you farewell, go in peace.

Yemoja to Protect a Child

As a youth in New York City, I had to be alert to many dangers. The most dangerous temptation of all was peer pressure. I saw many good kids from excellent homes led astray. Now, I'm not sure about other parts of the country, but the pressure to conform to the status quo in New York was high.

One day a kid was getting teased for being nerdy and getting straight A's. The next day that same kid was running with a gang, missing school, and acting like a major delinquent. But that's what happened to the ones who were lucky. You could turn them back with some intervention.

The not so fortunate ones faced a hell of torment. Once they were deemed "corny," it was downhill from there. They were the kids who crumpled in on themselves. They were the students who were attacked and ostracized. We now know the long-term effects this kind of treatment can have on a child. We understand the ramifications all too well. But back then, these norms were accepted by the kids, educators, and parents.

In my school, there was one boy in particular who evoked my sense of empathy. On the first day of school, he looked excited and energetic. He was dressed perfectly and radiated contentment. You could tell that his family cared for him. But someone identified him as a target for ridicule. Unfortunately, he didn't know how to stand up for himself.

By the end of the week, he was bullied so much, he ended up in the teacher's office hiding and crying. At the close of the month, he looked haggard and disheveled. Finally, before the school year concluded, he had a vacant hollowed-eye look in his eyes. His grades were low, and his attendance was even lower. I think that by then he had completely given up on trying. He looked like he just wanted it to end.

Ladies, this is one of the most infuriating things about life: the fact that you could birth a child in joy, raise him or her with tender care and compassion, and set the child on what you believe to be the right path only for some monster/s to take it upon themselves to attack and destroy the beautiful child you created. I saw this happen so many times I lost count. I want you to be aware of the dangers to your children.

If you know your child is facing bullying or ostracism, I want you to think twice about dismissing the situation as petty growing pains. I've seen and heard parents do this. They may say to their child, "You don't need any friends" or "Don't follow the crowd" or "Just wait until you grow up, you'll show them." These sayings don't help. They don't alleviate the pain and damage bullying causes.

Listen to your children. Pay attention if their moods and behaviors suddenly change. Take action to keep them safe, happy, and whole. You can ask Yemoja to help protect your child. Earlier in the book, we used her energy to calm and soothe. However, she can also be a fierce protector. She's the Orisha of the sea, but motherhood is also her domain.

You will need

- ❀ Four blue candles
- ❀ Three white candles
- ❀ Frame

- Image of Yemoja

- Large bowl of water (a beautiful one if you have it)

- 7 white roses (cut the stems off leaving the roses intact)

Procedure

1. Set the picture into the frame and set it in the center of your altar.

2. Place the bowl of water in front of the picture.

3. Set the seven candles around the bowl.

4. Light the candles.

5. Now call to Yemoja with these words:

Yemoja, Yemayá, Iemoja mother of all living things, she who rules over motherhood and owns all the waters of the Earth. She who gave birth to the stars, the moon, the sun and most of the Orishas, I call to you. Send your spirit, Oh Yemoja. Send your spirit to protect my child, [name of child]. Yemoja, Yemayá, Iemoja mother of all living things, she who rules over motherhood and owns all the waters of the Earth. She who gave birth to the stars, the moon, the sun, and most of the Orishas. Cover her/him with your protection so that she/he is guarded from all attacks. Oh, Yemoja, Yemayá, Iemoja mother of all living things, she who rules over motherhood and owns all the waters of the Earth. She who gave birth to the stars, the moon, the sun and most of the Orishas, I thank you. I leave this as an offering in thanks for your assistance.

6. Place the roses in the bowl of water.

7. Work this ritual for seven days. Then let the candles burn down and dispose of the items in a river.

Protective Charm

This is a great method to provide protection for you or a loved one. You should be employing many different methods of protection. I love using the pentagram for protection. I once believed that it was a symbol of the Devil and of evil. Imagine my surprise when I learned of its true origins?

Once I found out that the pentagram was a symbol of protection, I began to put it on everything I owned. I drew it on my shoes, my jewelry, my front door, and even on my dog.

You will need

- Carnation – for protection
- Cinnamon – for protection and power
- Dill – for protection
- Coconut chips – for purification and protection
- Flaxseed – for protection
- Parchment or unlined paper
- Small drawstring bag
- High-quality red ink

- Alcohol
- Dragon's blood resin
- Felt tip pen for writing
- Frankincense Incense

Procedure

1. Ground and center.

2. Cast a circle and call the four quarters.

3. Light the incense.

4. You'll be making dragon's blood ink. This is simple enough. Just crush the dragon's blood resin in a mortar. Once it reaches the right consistency, mix with the red ink and add a couple drops of alcohol.

5. Then dip your felt pen into the ink and begin to draw a pentagram on the paper. As you draw each line, say the following:

   Pentagram, pentacle, your protection, I invoke!

6. Once you have completed the drawing, allow the ink to dry. Next, fold the paper three times. Fold it in half toward you then turn it slightly clockwise and fold it again. Repeat again until you've folded it three times.

7. Add the ingredients one by one to the drawstring bag. Once you've finished, tie five knots to seal the bag. Finally, hold the bag over the incense while imaging it repelling all negativity. The charm is ready for use.

Incantation for Safe Travel

Have you ever taken a trip where everything went wrong? Maybe the pilot was late, delaying the plane for hours? Or perhaps the airline mixed up your tags and your bags were sent to the wrong destination? Traveling can be an exciting experience but there are many things you can't account for. For example, I have a friend whose meticulously planned summer getaway was ruined by an unexpected storm. Her flight was canceled because the adverse weather was deemed too dangerous for flight. While she complained, I thought she was lucky the airline came to this decision before the plane was actually in the sky. Here's a helpful incantation you can use when you travel to make sure you're lucky, too!

> *Abeona, Goddess of Outward Journeys,*
> *My travels have just begun.*
> *See that I arrive safely,*
> *Guide quickly to my destination.*
> *When my trip is done,*
> *Abeona, take me back*
> *Once I've had my fun!*

Deconstructed Witch's Bottle Centerpiece to Protect the Home

Ancient folklore is full of tales of small creatures or spirits that inhabit homes and assist the occupants of that home. Well, I'm here to tell you that it's true! Whether you want to call them angels, Earth spirits, brownies, ancestors, or fairies know that they're real. And we can reach out to them for their aid in many matters of the home. In this ritual we'll create a witch's protection bottle of sorts and ask our home spirits to empower it.

You will need

- Large decorative glass bowl or vase
- Plate or container
- Spoon
- Stick of incense of your choice
- Salt
- Rosemary – for protection and to ward off evil
- Lavender – to bring peace
- Purple geraniums – for protection and peace (white can be used)
- Dried blueberries – to keep negative people away from your home and protect against evil
- Mimosa – guards against hexes, curses, and future problems
- Caraway seeds – for protection against evil spirits and theft
- Whole cinnamon sticks – for protective vibrations
- 3-4 medium sized quartz or amethyst crystal points (can use quartz crystal chips instead)
- Blue and red food coloring

Procedure

1. First assemble the items for this spell at your altar.

2. Ground and center.

3. Cast a circle and call the four quarters.

4. Pour salt into container. It should be enough salt to completely cover the bottom or your decorative glass bowl.

5. Add red and blue food coloring to the salt one drop at a time, stirring until the salt turns a lovely shade of light purple.

6. Next, place the salt into the decorative bowl/vase.

7. Add the caraway seeds, dried blueberries, rosemary and lavender, layering them as you go.

8. Next, burrow the cinnamon stick into the piece but allow the top to protrude.

9. Then, sprinkle the geraniums and mimosa over the herbs.

10. Finally, stand the crystal points on top of the salt and herbs by burying the base of the point into the mixture.

11. Once you have assembled the piece, charge it by stating the following:

Spirits of hearth and home, I seek your presence this day. Hear my call, hear my request. I charge you to empower this sacred vessel for protection of my home and all who reside within. House spirits come and empower this vessel; empower this vessel now, I charge you. Please accept this incense in thanks (light incense). I thank you for your assistance and bid you farewell.

12. Allow the vessel to sit at your altar over night or for twenty-four hours.

13. When you're ready, place it in the center of your home.

Chapter 9

Success Spells

Opportunity now flows to me
like water in a stream.

The concept of success varies wildly depending on who you ask as the very notion is one that's deeply personal to our individual hopes and aspirations. However, many hurdles to success are common. In my opinion, the most common obstacle to success is a lack of belief in one's self. It becomes infinitely easier to acquire the job, pass that exam, start that business or finish that book once you develop an unshakable belief in yourself and your abilities. Once you have strengthened the belief in yourself, let this magic work to bring your efforts into fruition, and then allow yourself to celebrate your success.

Durga for Winning Spirit

Have you ever felt tired of fighting? I know I have. In my youth, I took meeting with resistance in stride and felt a strong fighting spirit urging me on towards my goals. However, I grew up and faced numerous disappointments and failures; I became somewhat disillusioned and felt in danger of losing that spark. I knew I had to do something about it. Perhaps you feel as though you've lost the fiery spark that drives you to overcome life's challenges. Or maybe your go-getter attitude has dulled over the years. If so, then read on because the ritual below may help you reclaim your lost vigor.

Durga was the first Hindu goddess I worked with back in the day. The feeling of her power is amazing. If you don't know, she's a warrior goddess known for defeating demonic forces. She's depicted with many arms. She sits astride a lion and uses it to trample her enemies. She's famed for killing the buffalo demon Mahishasura. Even while fighting demonic forces she remains calm, cool and collected. Thus, her warrior nature is shown to be a natural manifestation of protective motherhood.

In this ritual, you'll be tapping into her tranquil warrior nature to empower yourself with the ability to face anything and win!

You will need

* Prayer beads – should be Buddhist prayer beads or malas with 108 beads
* Frame

- Picture of Durga (preferably showing her slaying an enemy)
- 2 candles

Procedure

1. Ground and center.

2. Cast a circle and call the four quarters.

3. This is a simple ritual where you'll be chanting Durga's mantra: *Om Dum Durgayae Namaha*

4. Place the picture in the frame and set it between the two candles. Light your incense and candles.

5. Center yourself, and then begin chanting.

6. Hold the prayer beads in your hand as you chant.

7. Repeat the mantra for each bead until you have completed one round.

8. As you chant, envision yourself as Durga, with her many arms, slaying her enemies with skill and determination. Merge with her and feel yourself having that power within you.

Tarot Spell to Pass an Exam

We've all become a little anxious before a big test, job presentation or interview. But, of course, it's something you have to overcome. My latest test happened when I decided to become a certified expert in Photoshop, an ACE. What does it mean to be an ACE? It means that you've proven that you have a certain level of proficiency in Photoshop. It was both a personal and professional goal. You see, I was planning to ask for a much-needed salary increase. And I thought that this would be the icing on the cake of my stellar job performance.

If you know anything about Photoshop, then you understand how complex the software is. And by this point, I'd been out of school for over seven years and felt like I forgot how to prep for an exam. But, when I started using Photoshop a year prior, I knew absolutely nothing. By the end of the year, I was creating impressive images, greeting cards, invitations, marketing materials, and brochures, so I was ready to take on this challenge. I just needed a little boost of confidence. Luckily, I had magic on my side. And I decided to use it to give myself an edge while studying. Of course, I think you should, too. Are you studying for an important exam and want to increase your odds of success? Then performing the ritual below may help you.

You will need

- ❀ Chariot tarot card – for willpower and moving steadily toward your goals
- ❀ Yellow candle – for intellectual matters and improving mental powers
- ❀ Almond oil – for wisdom
- ❀ Green Aventurine – mental powers and luck

Timing

On a Sunday or Tuesday, Moon in Virgo

Procedure

1. Lay the chariot card on your altar. Anoint the candle with the almond oil then place the candle behind the tarot card. Put the aventurine on top of the chariot card.

2. In your mind, see yourself studying for the exam. Make it as detailed as possible. See yourself, perhaps with a spotlight above. See your books and materials scattered around you.

3. Next, see yourself sitting for the exam, confidently answering questions. There's a sense of ease about you.

4. Say the following:

   I'm prepared for the coming examination.
   With rigor and focus, my knowledge deepens.
   When the time comes, I'll show,
   What I've learned, what I know.
   When I walk out of this test,
   I'll smile, confident I've done my best!

5. Let the candle burn down. Keep the aventurine stone with you when you study or prepare for your big day. Take the stone with you on the big day. If your nerves start to act up, hold the stone in your hand and think of how you worked your ass off to get to this point.

Tarot Spell for Business Success

Being self-employed is one of the most rewarding things you can do for yourself. However, your success hinges on many unknown and unknowable factors. If you're self-employed, you know what I'm talking about. There's always a certain level of anxiety because you have to account for everything. How do you effectively market your product or service? What is your target demographic? How should you price your product or service to ensure you stay competitive without short-changing yourself?

Let's engage in a short story time. This story is about Christina, who is actually a friend of a friend. She's a very bright and determined Black woman. After years of working for an accounting firm, she decided to set up shop on her own. She assumed it would be easy to find clients because she has a large family, many friends, and many connections. She figured that business from friends and family would hold her over until she secured larger, real clients. That approach worked for a while, as friends and family sent business her way. She had substantially lower prices than competitors so people flocked to her.

Unfortunately, this decision came back to bite her on her ass. You see, after a few years of offering ridiculously low prices, she realized how much money she'd let slip through her fingers. So, she decided to raise her prices to reflect market rates. And of course, she lost a lot of business. To make matters worse, her low prices actually worked to deflect larger potential clients from her business.

This story illustrates just some of the unforeseen problems that can occur when you're self-employed. How can you prevent the unforeseen? Well, you can't. But you can use magic to attract business success to help you weather any storm and come out mostly unscathed. If you have a business, want to start a business, work as a freelancer, or have a side hustle, you can try the ritual below to increase your chances for success.

You will need

- Sun tarot card – for achievement
- The Emperor tarot card – for mastery
- Three of Wands tarot card – for growth, expansion, and manifestation
- The King of Pentacles tarot card – for wealth, business, security, and abundance
- Green candle – for growth
- Olive Oil – for blessings
- Kelp – to attract business
- Citrine chips (real not heat-treated) – to symbolize wealth
- Business card or something that is specific to your business like a branded item

Procedure

1. Ground and center.

2. Cast a circle and call the four quarters.

3. With your intent firmly in mind, lay out the cards. Place the cards in the following manner- The Sun, The Emperor, The Three of Wands, The King of Pentacles. Take a minute to study them and let the images sink into your consciousness.

4. Hold the green candle in your hand and imaging your business prospering and growing. As you do so, anoint the candle with the olive oil and apply the kelp. Place the green candle in the center of the spread and light the candle. Put your business card on top of the tarot cards.

5. Take the citrine chips and scatter them over the cards and around the candle.

6. State the following:

    The sun, the emperor, the three of wands, the king of pentacles (Touch each card in turn),

    Now hear this charge:
    Bring my business abundant success (Touch your hand to the business card).
    The flow of clients shall have no rest.
    Give mastery of the four elements:
    Fire, Water, Air, and Earth.
    To bless my business development,
    As I will it, so it shall be!

Work this spell for three days. Then allow the candle to burn down.

Crystal and Herb-Infused Water for Discipline

To achieve anything, you need the discipline to follow up word with deed. Having lofty goals is a fine thing. But do you know how to take action? How can you stay the course? How do you keep pushing even when things get tough? Be honest. But what's discipline? There are many definitions, but the ones below stand out.

- training that corrects, molds, or perfects the mental faculties or moral character ("Discipline," Merriam-Webster, 2019)

- to train or develop by instruction and exercise especially in self-control ("Discipline," Merriam-Webster, 2019)

- self-control ("Discipline," Merriam-Webster, 2019)

We often lack the discipline it takes to achieve our goals. Then we turn around and blame our lack of success on racism, sexism, classism, our past, our upbringing, or our mommas and daddies. We don't see where we slacked off, where we could have pushed harder. And then when we fail, we become full of disappointment, resentment, and shame.

Tamika, a friend from college was exactly like this: she lacked the discipline it took to reach her goals. I'd watch her quietly from the corner of my eye whenever we studied together. The girl would constantly get distracted, by her phone, her makeup, her food. When she had to write a research paper, she'd gather the books around her, preparing to get to work, but then she'd suddenly feel like a nap five minutes later and doze off on her books.

She isn't the only Black woman or person I know who lacks discipline. I see one in the mirror every day when I can't seem to remember where I left my keys. And I'm sure that if you're honest with yourself, you'll admit that there are areas of your life where you suffer from a lack of discipline. It could be something small, like not getting up early enough to exercise even though you want to lose weight. Or possibly a larger issue, like not remembering to pay a bill on time. Whatever it is, I'll tell you this: A lack of discipline will catch up to you in life. It did with Tamika. She did finish college, but it took her two additional years in school to get her degree. A massive delay in her life. And, ladies, we don't have years to waste on foolishness. So, if you're lacking in discipline, get real with yourself and admit it, then perform this ritual. And drink this infusion to keep yourself on track.

You will need

- Spearmint leaves – to sharpen mental powers
- Onyx – for self-discipline
- A glass water bottle

Procedure

1. Ground and center.

2. Cast a circle and call the four quarters.

3. Hold the onyx in your hands and think of your goal. See yourself putting in the work to achieve this goal;

happily. Feel the determination rise up within in you, then say:

Stone of power, stone of might,
Grant me discipline, to win my fight.
Strengthen my determination from within,
Strengthen my will, to secure the win

4. Hold the spearmint leaves in your hand and empower them with your intention.

5. Put the bottle in a sunny place so that it is charged by the sun.

6. Drink throughout the day

7. Add the spearmint into the glass bottle

8. Pour water into a bowl and add the onyx

9. Place the water bottle with the mint into the bowl so that it is infused with the energy of the stone

10. Remove water bottle after 6-12 hours and toss out water in the bowl (do not drink this water as it could be toxic)

Chapter 10

Arts and Spellcraft

I'm propelled forward to my desires.

I've loved arts and crafts as a kid and I still do. There's always a new project on my mind. In fact, being a witch has served to increase my creativity. Let us not forget that we're practicing witch*craft.* This means that from the outset our intention is to use the energy of the universe to create what we desire for ourselves. Creation is what this journey is all about. So, we should always be tapped into the energy of creation. And below are some useful spell craft ideas that will help you flex that creative muscle. Don't forget that these can be used as inspiration for your own crafts. You can tweak and adjust any element to make them your own.

Astrological Spell Candle

Witches and candles are an inseparable duo. My first spell was a candle spell, and it was basic. When I first started out, I didn't know what to do and I didn't have a clue where to begin. I understand why so many new witches are confused. You have to figure everything out on your own.

So that's what I did. I started with candle magic. I went to the nearest craft store and walked through the candle aisle. My head spun as I looked at the different colors and sizes. In the end, I decided to keep it simple and reached for the white candle. When I got home, I proceed to perform my ritual. I had some serious doubts about the ritual because it was deceptively simple. But I put my doubts aside, finished the ritual and went on with my life. Within days I saw the results. Now I incorporate candles into many of my spells.

Eventually, I got the great idea to make my own candles. It's not a radically new idea, people have been making their own candles for ages. The process is simple, and the benefits are great. You can add any scent you like. You can use fresh or dried flowers, or you could enchant the wax and the wick. Whatever you choose to do, do it cautiously. The hot water and wax can, of course, burn you. Certain herbs and essential oils are harmful to different groups. So, please, before you attempt the candle-making ritual below, make sure that you have set your workspace properly to minimize risk. It's also your responsibility to investigate any ingredient shown before you use it.

In essence, the candle-making ritual below is fun and engaging.

You will need

- ❀ Paraffin wax chips (1 pound will make four 6 oz. candles)
- ❀ Wicks
- ❀ Wick sticky tabs (available in craft stores)
- ❀ Pot
- ❀ Heat-resistant container (Pyrex measuring cup will do)
- ❀ Thermometer - to monitor wax temperature
- ❀ Wooden stick
- ❀ Candle mold or glass jar/container
- ❀ Yellow food coloring
- ❀ Blue and gold glitter
- ❀ Bergamot essential oil

Procedure

1. Secure the wick to the center of the candle mold or glass container using the wick sticky tabs.

2. Fill the pot halfway with water. Slowly heat the water (don't let it boil). Then carefully place the pyrex cup with wax chips into the water. Allow the wax to melt slowly. Once the wax is completely melted, remove the pot from the stove.

3. Next, into the melted wax add 5 drops of bergamot oil and yellow food coloring. Carefully remove the Pyrex of melted wax from the pot.

4. Slowly pour the wax into the mold or glass jar. Now add the glitter, alternating blue and gold. You could also use a toothpick to swirl the glitter into the wax.

5. Roll the wick around the wooden stick to keep it in place as the wax sets. Leave the candle in a cool dry place for 24 hours.

6. After the candle has solidified, etch the Gemini astrological symbol on the side of the candle.

7. Anoint with almond oil before use.

Yemoja Beaded Necklace for Protection

I love wearing my magic and I love creating. So, it's only natural that I would eventually find a way to combine the two. A beaded necklace is one of the simplest kinds of jewelry you can make. Once you're done, you can either wear it yourself or give it as a gift to a loved one.

You will need

* White beads (I prefer crystal beads and they are technically considered white)
* Blue beads
* Blue rope necklace

Procedure

1. Ground and center.

2. Cast a circle and call the four quarters.

3. Sit quietly and think of the sea. Imagine calming soothing waters. Feel the immense power of the ocean. Know that this power can surround you and protect you as water once guarded you in the womb.

4. Now add the beads in the following pattern; 7 white beads, then 7 blue beads, then 7 white and 7 blue until all are on the necklace.

5. As you work, chant the following:

    Yemoja, protector of women, fertility, motherhood, grant your protection.

Once complete, wear the necklace whenever you wish to feel her motherly protection.

Miniature Poppet to Retain Youth and Beauty

When I decided to dive into creating and using dolls, I was initially a little worried about the possible repercussions. I was a little worried about the karma (no such thing) and how messing with a 'voodoo doll' could possibly backfire on me. Of course, I know now that the karma nonsense is just a bunch of bull. But at the time I thought I'd play it safe by using this magic to make changes to myself. Magic used to make self-changes has the greatest effect on our lives and this one didn't disappoint.

You will need

- Two 12 inch pink pipe cleaners
- Pink and white yarn
- Salt water

Procedure

1. Take items to your altar.

2. Ground and center.

3. Cast circle and call four quarters.

4. Take one pipe cleaner and bend it in half.

5. Create a loop by placing two fingers through the bend

6. Now, twist just below the bend to secure the loop. You should now have a loop that looks like a head on one end and two hanging ends.

7. Next, take the second pipe cleaner and bend the two ends towards the center creating two loops, one on either end. These will be the two arms of the poppet.

8. Use the extra length to secure the arms just below the head loop by wrapping them around until they create a little 'chest'

9. Next, create the legs by making two additional loops with the hanging length of the pipe cleaner used to form the head.

10. Take a 12 inch length of the pink and white yarn and cut them into two inch pieces.

11. Wrap one of the pieces through the head loop and knot it to secure the piece. This is the hair of the poppet. Repeat until you are satisfied with the amount of hair.

12. Once the little poppet is created, you need to baptize it. Take the salt water, sprinkle it on the poppet while saying the following:

    I baptize you as [name] by Earth, air, fire and water. Your purpose is to retain and magnify my youthful beauty. You'll constantly work to achieve your purpose. By the power of earth, air, fire and water I breathe life into you, I command you to live now and go out to fulfill your purpose. Go now, go. As I will it, so let it be.

13. Keep your poppet on your vanity (or wherever you apply your makeup) and periodically speak to it, telling it how beautiful it is and speaking words of affirmation.

Please note, that you could make a poppet like this for any issue by simply switching out the color.

Chapter 11

Miscellaneous

*In the end, I will complete this magical
journey with a smile on my face and
a whispered thanks on my lips.*

For this section, I've added some spells and rituals that while useful don't fit into the other chapters of this book. These are no less important than anything that has come before it.

Communication Oil

The ability to communicate clearly makes life easier. Whether you're a student, educator, office drone, or entrepreneur, you can benefit from strengthening your communication skills. In small everyday matters like ordering coffee and going to the cleaners to more significant matters such as giving a presentation or negotiating a contract, your ability to communicate can greatly affect the outcome.

Many people forget that communication is a two-way street. They may also fail to understand what is **not** being said. They might not pick up on certain signs or misinterpret what's said.

My friend Jennifer, whom I love, is a little scatterbrained and lacks both understanding and clarity. Additionally, she has the unfortunate habit of pretending to know more than she actually does. These qualities are a recipe for disaster. When Jennifer landed a new job, she failed to read the fine print on the contract. She was so wrapped up in looking good to the prospective employer, that she barely listened to what the boss had to say. She didn't think to ask the right questions. So, it came as a shock to her that the contract would begin nearly two months after she left her current position.

The two-month waiting period would put a great deal of financial strain on her, but she pretended she knew about the start date and signed the contract anyway. She then proceeded to complain about not having a steady source of income and having to "struggle."

When she moved to a new city, she missed out on getting into one of the higher floors in a high-rise building. The rental agent's understanding of English was poor, so when the agent asked Jennifer whether Americans considered the number 13 bad luck, Jennifer said yes. Jennifer then thoroughly explained why Americans consider 13 bad luck, the origin of the superstition, and a discourse on Jesus and his disciples. She was so busy playing the expert that she didn't read between the lines. The agent was trying to test her understanding of what Jennifer wanted, but Jen missed the implication.

The rental agent began to show her apartments on the ground floor. Sure, the agent was equally at fault. But had Jennifer asked questions to clarify and not try to seem like an expert, she could have got an apartment with a great view instead of the ground-floor, back-facing apartment she has now.

Ladies, don't be like Jennifer. Polish and hone your communication skills so that you don't miss out on life's great opportunities. This communication oil recipe could give you the extra boost you need to do just that.

You will need

- Almond oil – almonds are used for wisdom and are connected to Mercury and element of air
- 3 drops bergamot essential oil – for clarity (do not take internally)
- 3 drops lemongrass essential oil – for psychic powers (do not take internally)
- 4 Agate chips – for the courage to speak
- 4 Amethyst chips – for mental and psychic powers
- 4 Peridot chips – to guard against illusions and see clearly
- A few sprigs of rosemary – for mental powers
- Dark bottle

Timing

Wednesday, during a waxing or full moon

Procedure

1. Ground and center.

2. Cast a circle and call the four quarters.

3. State the following:

   Mercury, Roman messenger god, god who watches over trade and commerce, I invoke you. Mercury, come be with me now. Hear me, Mercury, and come to me. Mercury, god of travelers, boundaries, luck, trickery, merchants, thieves, I call to you. Mercury, he who holds the Caduceus in his left hand and wears winged sandals on his feet. Come, honor me with your presence. Hail to you, oh Mercury. Aid me in my endeavor!

4. Add the agate chips, the amethyst chips, the peridot chips, and the sprig of rosemary to the bottle. Next, pour in the almond oil to cover all the ingredients. To this add, 4 drops of bergamot essential oil and lemongrass essential oil. Next, put the sprig of rosemary into the bottle.

5. As you gently shake the bottle, say the following

   Add to this mix your gift of communication, oh Mercury. When I wear this may my words be sweet but powerful, direct but tactful, clear and precise. My mental capabilities will increase causing my clarity and understanding to grow.

Place the mixture in a cool dark place. You can you use it before a job interview, a presentation, a speech, before negotiating a raise, or even before a date.

Beauty Butter

Black don't crack. But that doesn't mean that we can neglect our beauty rituals. Did you know that you can give your beauty products a boost by enchanting them for their purpose? I've done it with excellent results. If you want your hair to shine, add a little magic to your shampoo and conditioner. Do you want healthy gleaming teeth? Then charm your toothpaste to supercharge its benefits. And if you want your beat face to look on point, then charm the hell out of your cosmetics and makeup tools. Enchanting your beauty items will make people wonder about your beauty secrets.

Even better, make your own beauty products from scratch. Use the great recipe below to create a beauty butter that will leave you looking flawless.

You will need

- Avocado oil – avocado pits are carried to promote beauty
- Flaxseed oil – to enhance beauty
- Ginseng – to bring beauty
- Raw mango butter

- Jasmine or rose essential oil - for scent
- Hot water
- Small glass bowl
- Lager glass bowl
- Plastic jar with cover
- Wooden spoon
- A length of pink cord/yarn – pink for love and beauty
- Small Venus symbol – for beauty

Timing

On a Friday night, during a waxing moon

Procedure

1. Ground and center.

2. Cast a circle and call the four quarters.

3. Place the smaller glass bowl in the center of the larger one.

4. Add the raw mango butter to the small bowl.

5. Pour the boiling hot water into the large bowl. The mango butter will begin to melt. Use the wooden spoon to help the process along until the butter has an almost liquid consistency.

6. Pour in the almond oil and a few drops of the essential oil. Add one or two drops of the ginseng. Add the Venus symbol.

7. Mix the ingredients together as you chant:

   Praise, praise, praise,
   This beauty balm, make me dazzle and amaze!

8. As the water cools, the mixture will begin to solidify. Before it does, take out the Venus symbol and clean it off thoroughly.

9. Gently and carefully pour the mixture into the plastic jar. Pour a little at a time to allow it to settle.

10. Allow it to cool.

11. Now take the pink cord and slip the Venus symbol on, so it's in the middle.

12. Then tie six knots and for each knot chant the following:

    By knot of one, the spell's begun.
    By knot of two, it'll be true.
    By knot of three, butter beautify me.
    By knot of four, my youth restore.
    By knot of five, the spell's alive.
    By knot of six, it's fixed!

13. Tie the cord around the bottle.

The spell is done. Apply as desired.

Pendulum Ritual to Discover Your Gifts

I bet you don't know everything you're capable of achieving. Perhaps you have the ability to be a painter or a violinist. Maybe you have what it takes to be a brilliant pastry chef or an inspiring poet? Whatever your gifts may be, don't you think you owe it to yourself to discover them?

My elderly next-door neighbor Simone did. When her husband passed, she was devastated. She didn't know what to do with herself for a year afterward. But one day I saw her coming in and greeted her. She looked livelier than she had for quite some time. I asked her what was new. She said she started to take a poetry class at a community center. Apparently, she had a real talent for writing poetry and enjoyed it immensely. But she never knew! Before long I started seeing her with a pencil and notebook, writing or muttering to herself. She told me that she wished she knew about her talent sooner; it could have helped her through some dark times, or she could've made some money from it.

You will need

- A crystal pendulum
- A pen
- A medium-sized circular object
- Paper

Procedure

1. Ground and center.

2. Cast a circle and call the four quarters.

3. Using the circular object, trace a circle. Draw a large X in the center dividing the circle into four quadrants.

4. In each quadrant, write one of the following; Intellectual, Creative, Physical, Spiritual.

5. Hold the crystal in your palm close your eyes, take three deep breaths and say the following:

   Magical crystal, charm of mine:
   Show me where true my talents lie.

6. With your eyes still closed, allow the crystal to dangle as you chant.

7. Slowly move your hand closer to the paper until you feel it connect.

8. Open your eyes,

9. Whichever quadrant the crystal rests on is where your secret talent lies.

10. You can use four different possible hobbies that fall under the heading of the quadrant you landed on then repeat the ritual again to whittle down your choices.

To Gain a New Perspective

I have to admit it: In my youth, I had some trouble interpreting facts. This was a shame because my skewed perspective colored everything I did. Plus, I could have avoided some very bad behavior and the adverse consequences. In my defense, I simply didn't know any better. But I definitely thought I did. I thought I knew so much.

So how can you tell if you have a skewed perspective that may be impacting your decisions and behavior? A simple test is to ask yourself if you think you know everything or know more than others. Do you ever think, "I know what I know and I'm right"? If so, you may benefit from a change of perspective. Your biases and assumptions may be clouding your judgment. And it matters, it matters a lot. Because you act out of these assumptions, you may turn down opportunities or head toward something that's completely wrong for you.

A former coworker named Rosa suffered from this very problem, but she couldn't see it, of course. She worked as trainer for the firm, helping new employees with onboarding and training staff on new technology. However, there was a problem: Rosa wasn't great at her job. She didn't have patience, and she struggled to provide clarity on issues. She often looked like she couldn't wait for training sessions to end. Many of the employees were unhappy with her performance. One day, we ran into each other during lunchtime and had lunch together.

Right away she started to complain about her job and aspects that were her basic duties! It became obvious to me that she was frustrated because she found it difficult to keep up with the changes in technology. She didn't understand them and couldn't adapt, so she became apathetic about her work. She would never admit that, of course. I'm not even sure she knew it herself. If she had some way to gain perspective on her situation, she might have been able to see that she was no longer a fit for her current role. And she had been with the company for 15 years by this point!

It's obvious that the way we view and interpret information has tangible effects on our lives. A change in perspective may help you to see yourself and the situations around you in a new light. It may take the blinders off your eyes and cause you to move in a new direction.

You will need

- ❀ A quartz crystal – to open you to spiritual experiences
- ❀ Bay leaves – for dreams
- ❀ Jasmine – for dreams
- ❀ Rose incense – for scent
- ❀ Blue sachet

Procedure

1. Ground and center.

2. Cast a circle and call the four quarters.

3. Just before bed, burn the rose incense.

4. Place the items in the sachet.

5. Press the sachet to your forehead and say the following:

   Crystal, bay, and jasmine shine.
   A light in this stubborn mind of mine.
   Allow to me see, what may be,

Tonight, bring fresh ideas to me!

6. Sleep with the sachet under your pillow.

To Prevent Mistakes, Mishaps, and Accidents

Mistakes happen. But if you seem to be accident-prone, you should take a good look at your own personal behavior first. Personal accountability is key in life. So, take a true assessment of yourself and ask yourself this question, "Am I a careless person?"

What do I mean by careless? The dictionary definition is "not giving sufficient attention or thought to avoiding harm or errors." ("Careless," Lexico.com 2019) There you have it. Someone not paying enough attention will cause harm and errors.

How frequently have you rushed to get on a train only to realize you're going in the wrong direction? How many times are you caught in the rain without an umbrella? How often do you miss your exit on the road? All are failures of attention.

How often have you got turned around when meeting friends and arrived late? If you weren't careless, you would've planned how to get to your destination before you left the house. You may be careless if you've ever left your house without **knowing** (not just guessing or being pretty sure), where you're going, how long it will take to get there, what means of transportation you'll use, and how you'll return.

If you've ever shown up at an event over- or under-dressed, you may be careless and oblivious.

If you don't pay attention to street signs to guide your way, you may be careless. If your boss seems to be getting on your case more than anyone else's, you may be careless. You see, most accidents and mistakes can be avoided by doing things with care and focused attention.

So, this is a spell to prevent mistakes and accidents by working to improve your attention.

You will need

- The fool tarot card – to represent our foolishness
- A black candle
- An image of Nyd -- the banishing rune (can be found on the web.)

Timing

On Saturday, during a waning moon

Procedure

1. Ground and center.

2. Cast a circle and call the four quarters.

3. Look at the fool tarot card. Notice how carefree the fool looks. Recognize how his face is tilted upward, toward the sky. He doesn't see the road ahead and hasn't planned for it. He's wandering aimlessly toward his certain doom, with a smile on his face.

4. Now know that this is you, mistake- and accident-prone because of the same carelessness. Every time you're hit with the unexpected because of not preparing. Every time the people around you suffer due to your negligence, realize that you're playing the fool.

5. Take your candle in hand and feel a strong sense of determination. Determination that you'll never play the fool again. Feel it strongly. You're sending away that careless little girl for good.

6. With a pin, carve Nyd, the banishing rune, into the black candle. Do so with the intent of banishing in mind.

7. Light the black candle. Hold the fool card and say the following:

Careless heart, careless mind
Foolish girl, wasting time.
I release you, I don't need you.
I release you and will not feed you.
Go now go, you're not welcome within.
Go now go, take your careless, childish whims.
Light the fool card and allow it to burn in a fire-proof pot.

8. Sprinkle a pinch of the ashes into the flame and say the following:

Foolish little girl in me, I bid you farewell.
With this candle you're banished.
Once it melts, you'll be dead!

Bibliography

Angel Magic: A Hands-on Guide to Inviting Divine Help into Your Everyday Life, Cassandra Eason

Encyclopedia of Magical Herbs, Scott Cunningham

The Voodoo Hoodoo Spell Book, Denise Alvarado

A Guide to Serving the Seven African Powers, Denise Alvarado

The Woman's Dictionary of Symbols and Sacred Objects, Barbara G. Walker

The Spellcaster's Reference: Magical Timing for the Wheel of the Year, Eileen Holland

A Book of Pagan Ritual Prayer, Ceisiwr Serith

A Treatise on Angel Magic, Adam McLean

A Dictionary of Angels: Including the Fallen Angels, Gustav Davidson

Encyclopedia of Goddesses and Heroines, Patricia Monaghan

Modern Witchcraft Grimoire: Your Complete Guide to Creating Your Own Book of Shadows, Skye Alexander

Modern Witchcraft Grimoire Book of the Tarot: Your Complete Guide to Understanding the Tarot, Skye Alexander

Indian Mythology: Tales, Symbols, and Rituals from the Heart of the Subcontinent, Devdutt Pattanaik

Ganesha, Tamarapu Sampath Kumaran

A Comprehensive List of Gods and Goddesses of Ancient Egypt, compiled and edited by L.C.F

Cord Magic, Raven Willow

The Way of Orisa: Empowering Your Life Through the Ancient African Religion of Ifa, Philip John Neimark

Cerridwen, A-Museing Grace Gallery —The Magical Art of Thalia Took http://www.thaliatook.com/AMGG/cerridwen.php

Isis The Egyptian Goddess, https://www.goddessguide.com/isis.html

Top 10 Tarot Cards For Success And Achievement, Biddy Tarot https://www.biddytarot.com/top-10-tarot-cards-for-success-and-achievement/

7 Chakras: What Is A Chakra? How to Balance Chakras for Beginners, Katherine Hurst http://www.thelawofattraction.com/7-chakras/

"Wealth" (2019). In *Merriam-Webster*. Retrieved from https://www.merriam-webster.com/dictionary/wealth?utm_campaign=sd&utm_medium=serp&utm_source=jsonld

"Power" (2019). In *Merriam-Webster*. Retrieved from https://www.merriam-webster.com/dictionary/power

"Prosperity" (2019). In *Merriam-Webster*. Retrieved from https://www.merriam-webster.com/dictionary/prosperity

"Careless" (2019). In Lexico.com. Retrieved from https://www.lexico.com/en/definition/careless

Newman, Randy, "Friends on the Other Side" *The Princess and the Frog*, performed by Keith David, Walt Disney Records, 2009.